WITHOUT DARKNESS

Biblical Companions for a
Modern Journey

HELEN GALLIVAN

VERITAS

First published 2007 by
Veritas Publications
7/8 Lower Abbey Street
Dublin 1
Ireland
Email publications@veritas.ie
Website www.veritas.ie

ISBN 978 1 84730 053 9

10 9 8 7 6 5 4 3 2 1

All scripture quotations, unless otherwise indicated, taken from the *New Revised Standard Version Bible* © 1989 and 1995 by the Division of Christian Education of the National Churches of Christ in the United States of America.

Lines from Mary Oliver's 'In Blackwater Woods' taken from *American Primitive*, courtesy of Back Bay Books, 1983. Lines from R.S. Thomas's 'Kneeling' taken from *Poems*, courtesy of Phoenix, 2002. Lines from Rainer Maria Rilke's 'The Man Watching' from the translation by Robert Bly, taken from *The Rag and Bone Shop of the Heart*, courtesy of Harper Perennial, 1993.

A catalogue record for this book is available from the British Library.

Printed in the Republic of Ireland by Betaprint, Dublin

Veritas books are printed on paper made from the wood pulp of managed forests. For every tree felled, at least one tree is planted, thereby renewing natural resources.

TO PAUL,
DEAREST COMPANION

CONTENTS

❦

INTRODUCTION
TRAVELLING LIGHT

Journeys have a beginning and an end, but this journey began at the end – for the last chapter was written first. It started with the final stages of an earthly journey whose end was marked by pain, fear and extreme spiritual desolation. The courage with which that particular life had been lived had, it seemed, finally run out. A gallant and resilient person, who rejoiced in the happiness of others and who was never without a kind or cheerful word when hurt or sadness visited others, who bravely rose many times from the wreck of age and injury, had sustained one blow too many. Rigid with sorrow, I asked myself what had been sown to reap so bitter a harvest.

In those long vigil hours, I made the most unexpected acquaintance. I gazed across the space of two millennia and met Simon of Cyrene, another person bent under a cross not his own and on what appeared to be a similarly hopeless journey. As I retraced Simon's journey, I found myself with another singular travelling companion, St John of the Cross, whose description of a soul travelling in darkness led me to look in a new way at Simon's journey and, ultimately, at the journey whose end I was witnessing.

The journey made by us, from birth to death and rebirth, has been made over and over again for 50,000 years. Wastes that seem trackless have been crossed already. While nobody can make the journey for us, we do not need to make it alone. However, in the western world we are probably more alone now than at any other stage in our history.

In a time of enormous change, a connectedness with the past is vital if we are to maintain stability. The cult of the individual has never been so prominent and the quest for personal identity never so elusive. In the past, our identity sprang naturally from the culture, tradition, religion and sense of place that shaped our community. Now, the focus on our rights as individuals takes precedence over our sense of responsibility to others, and – far from enriching our lives – curiously reduces them. We compete rather than cooperate, learn in order to earn, consume rather than create.

We are no longer connected in the way even our most recent ancestors were with the place where we were born and grew up. Even our sense of family is affected by increased mobility, and by growing volatility in relationships. We are increasingly likely to live alone, especially as we get older.

In our solipsist isolation, the notion of drawing from a shared past has become alien to us. We can, however, become possessed by our own past, our own past failures especially, which drain us of confidence in our ability to move forward.

Through all of this, Simon of Cyrene made darkness visible for me and made a crooked way straight. Revisiting the pages of Scripture, I found myself part of an ancient community of memory. I found that the biblical 'family' is my family; the places are my places; the story is my story. The journey I walk has been walked by countless others. Like any other journey into the unknown, it helps to have a guide – someone who has gone that way before.

The Bible, bought by many but read by few, provided me with many other travelling companions in times of confidence and terror, exhilaration and discouragement, self-love and self-loathing, clarity and confusion. The people I encountered in the pages of the Bible are an extraordinary collection – ranging from wholly lovable to deeply unpleasant. Their journeys incorporate elements which embrace the tragic and the uplifting, the terrible and the playful. In their quest for integrity and identity they overcome self-deception, crippling fear, extreme vacillation, a longing to return to the comforts of slavery; they also demonstrate brutal honesty, dogged determination and stoical courage. All have this in common – the experiences these people lived, the conflicts they encountered, the routes they mapped, are as relevant today as they were when their stories were first told.

In walking different stages of my own life's journey in this varied company, I learned to shed baggage as I went. With Eve and with Mary, I made the exhilarating discovery that my journey is endlessly beginning and that I have the possibility of 'making my own soul' every day of my life. Birth and rebirth are an astonishing adventure in which the soul never ages. Even the aging of the body does not diminish our possibilities.

We are as much slaves today to false gods as anyone in the Old Testament. With Moses I learned that, to find my direction, I needed to go where there are no paths. The 'wilderness' is the place we must enter naked and silent, without food or drink, sex, drugs or deadlines, safety nets or empty spiritual practices. It is only in our interior landscape that the power of false gods must be broken – even though life without them may seem unimaginable to us.

Jonah reinforces how easy it is to find a boat going in the wrong direction! Like Jonah, I often turned away from what I knew I should do and sought safety in numbness. I found that it is possible to come back from the land of no return and to accept that being shaped by my past does not excuse me from changing direction in the future.

Lot's wife brought home to me how easy it is to see life in terms of who we are, what we do and what we possess. Our energies go into preserving the illusion of control over all of this. Real freedom only comes with the realisation that, while we may not be able to change the way we feel, we can change the way we act. Lot may have felt terrified, but he did leave Sodom. His wife's refusal to believe herself capable of change destroyed her from within.

In the temple at Shiloh, Hannah's triumphant and prophetic canticle showed me how the ending of one story is always the beginning of another. In our children we must willingly become a channel for God's transformative work.

At Simon the Pharisee's table, the nameless woman who washed the feet of Jesus showed me a form of prayer that rocked every preconception I had. The notion that I might use this language to speak to God seemed unthinkable to me – yet the great mystic, St Teresa of Avila, said that in the Song of Solomon the Lord is teaching the soul how to pray.

The things that weighed me down were things that could be excised, albeit with difficulty: things like my own defects, my past mistakes and the constraints of my world view. Like Jacob on the banks of the Jabbok, I found that sheer doggedness could change my name too.

With David, 'dancing with all his might' in God's presence, I saw how prayer can be completely connected with the created world which is itself constantly being recreated. In the immense, lyrical poem in which God speaks to Job, my heart was lifted inside me. With David, with Job and with Peter on the Mount of the Transfiguration, I found I could exclaim, 'Lord, it is wonderful for me to be here!'

What all these stories have in common is that they feature a crisis, in the original sense of the word as 'a turning point' – something to be welcomed rather than feared, something that the philosopher Ivan Illich described as the 'the marvellous moment when people become aware of their self-imposed cages, and of the possibility of a different life'.[1] This richly varied company transformed my own journey in a way I could not have imagined and helped me to appreciate that the always-present possibilities of change are the most liberating things life has to offer.

NOTE

1   Ivan Illich, *The Right to Useful Unemployment*, London, Marion Boyars Publishers Ltd., 1996, p. 20.

I

FOREVER BECOMING

Eve and Mary

Man makes his own soul throughout all his earthly days.

Pierre Teilhard de Chardin, *The Divine Milieu*

My advent

Our first and only child was born at ten minutes to midnight on 23 December. I have always loved the season of Advent; that year, when I was expecting a Christmas baby, I found the Advent liturgies almost unbearably moving. In my yearning expectancy the great O Antiphons, with their longing and mounting impatience, resonated with me as never before.

It seemed to me that all the mystery of creation was contained within me – our love for each other made flesh in a new being, as God's love for us was made flesh in Christ. At six weeks, I had had a scan and the doctor pointed out the tiny shadow on the ultrasound. A miniscule flicker was our baby's heartbeat – the little, leaping flame of new life, and contained within me! Now, eight months later, my body's small tenant was almost ready to be born. I waited for the birth with heartstopping excitement. And, through these final days of pregnancy, the beautiful, sombre rhythms of the O Antiphons seemed almost the rhythms of life itself. They are sung as though with breath held, suffused with reverence and wonder. 'O come, o come' – the verb *veni* is repeated again and again,

> recalling an urgent eschatological prayer so ancient that it was offered in the native Aramaic by the earliest Christian Church ... It embodies the deep yearning of the exiles in the Babylonian captivity for freedom, of the post-exilic Jews for the restoration of former glories perhaps personified in the Messiah, and of the primitive Church for a speedy return of its ascended Master. It is an intense prayer epitomising all prayers whatever their content.[1]

The Advent Antiphons are among the oldest prayers of the Church, and they have even more ancient resonances of

> the Shema ... of a prayer that originated in Eretz Israel, of rabbinical exaltation of wisdom and prudence, of midrashic lore about the attributes of God, and of stories of life in bondage, exile, and diaspora.[2]

'O come, Lord Jesus' – the fervent request is as old as St Paul[3] and forms the penultimate verse of the book of Revelation and thus of the New Testament. All of these associations were with me in those final days. I felt as old as Eve, participating in the act of Creation.

I woke before dawn on the eve of Christmas Eve to the certain knowledge that our baby was on the way. Eighteen hours later, it seemed as though this baby would never be born. 'Labour' is accurately named. For many hours beforehand, contractions had been sweeping in like tidal waves, each one picking me up like a tiny piece of flotsam and bearing me down into a new tunnel of pain and exhaustion. I no longer believed that this cruel effort was going to produce anything at all. In the brief respites between contractions I withdrew from time and the world. Inexorably drawn back by the next wave, I was surprised to find myself still there.

And so it went on, hour after hour – wholly relentless, unavoidable. And then, stunning pain, pain to take the breath away, and I began to know fear. The urge to deliver the baby was relentless – but it seemed like an urge to self destruct. I could no more avoid it than I will be able to avoid death. Then the moment came when, at last, with a final crescendo of effort, our baby was there. I held her warm living body against me, looked into her astonishingly calm eyes and instantly, irrevocably, fell in love. She glided around my heartstrings like running water to crystallise there, so that my heart was no longer mine but from then on a part of her.

This, then, or something like it, Mary went through. In blood and sweat and pain she went through this most elemental of experiences, lying on the mud floor of an outhouse. In the words of the opening prayer of the Dawn Mass on Christmas Day, 'Almighty God ... your Eternal Word leaped down from heaven in the silent watches of the night, and now your Church is filled with wonder at the nearness of her God'. The maker of the universe passed through a female womb and lay helpless and beloved on his mother's breast as my baby did on mine. Mary must have gazed on the infant Jesus with the same wonder that mothers have felt since Eve bore the first child in creation. Her first baby, for every woman, is the first baby in the world. Nobody will have gone through a pregnancy and delivery exactly like hers. Ask any mother about her child's birth, and the story will be absolutely unique to that mother and that baby. Nobody will feel the same sense of wonder at this particular miracle of creation. Eve's shout of triumph after the birth of Cain still echoes down the millennia: 'I have produced a man with the help of the Lord' (Gen 4:1).

EVE AND MARY – SISTERS IN TRIUMPH

Triumph is not an emotion one readily associates with Eve. From the early Church Fathers to reformers like Wesley and Calvin, the view of Eve has been of a woman condemned to sorrow and subjection because of her sin. In describing Mary as the 'New Eve', the original Eve is seen as the antithesis of Mary; as a fourth-century hymn puts it, 'In Mary, the bowed head of Eve was raised'.[4] As early as the second century, St Justin brought out the contrast between Eve and Mary. The virgin Eve accepted the word of the serpent and gave birth to disobedience and death; the Virgin Mary received the word of the angel with joy, and through the power of the Holy Spirit gave birth to the Son of God.[5] 'And thus,' adds St Irenaeus, 'as the human race fell into bondage to death by means of a virgin, so it is rescued by a virgin; a virgin's disobedience is balanced by virginal obedience.'[6] Eve allowed herself to be beguiled into disobedience by a fallen angel; Mary listened to another angel and became the mother of the New Adam.

However, this view of Eve is incomplete. To focus on the contrasts is to ignore the fascinating similarities. Some are obvious: Eve is the 'mother of all who live' (Gen 3:20) and Mary is the universal mother. Each stood at the dawn of a new creation. A much less apparent resonance is that triumph in Eve's cry on the birth of Cain and the way it is echoed in Mary's glorious canticle at the time she visits Elizabeth. It is no coincidence that throughout the Christmas Octave the O Antiphons are followed each night by the exuberance of the Magnificat: 'For behold, henceforth all generations will call me blessed. For he who is mighty has done great things for me.'

So there is Mary, on Elizabeth's threshold, and on the threshold of the New Covenant of God with his people, carrying within her womb One 'who is and who was and who is to come, the Almighty' (Rev 1:8). She has no difficulty reconciling the lowliness of her status with the greatness of her calling, just as Eve's triumph is undimmed by her expulsion from Paradise.

In the Genesis account, Eve was God's last earthly creation before he rested on the seventh 'day'. As he created things in ascending order, Eve was arguably the apogee of his creation. He entrusts ongoing creation to his creatures. To the woman he gives an exceptional role. Every woman can experience the genesis of life. In a sense, every woman stands at the dawn of a new creation. The first words of the Bible, 'In the beginning', can be experienced directly by her.

THE MOTHERING CREATOR

This sharing of the divine act of creation is reinforced throughout the Old and New Testaments. Time and again, God's creative actions are referred to in terms of childbearing and delivery. In Deuteronomy 32:18 God reproaches Israel with the words: 'You were unmindful of the Rock that bore you; you forget the God that gave you birth.' In one of the lyrical passages from the book of Job, God asks, 'Who shut in the sea with doors when it burst out from the womb?' and again, 'From whose womb did the ice come forth, and who has given birth to the hoarfrost of heaven?' (Job 38:8, 29). In Isaiah 46:3 God says: 'Listen to Me, O house of Jacob, all the remnants of the house of Israel, you who have been borne by me from your birth, carried from the womb.'

With the image of God giving birth to his creation comes the extraordinarily moving depiction of God's maternal love. In Jeremiah 31:3, 20, foretelling the restoration of Ephraim (the ten northern tribes of Israel), God's language has all the tenderness of motherhood:

> I have loved you with an everlasting love; ...
> Is Ephraim my dear son?
> Is he my darling child?

In the sheer delight of motherhood I began to have some inkling of God's love for us. His tenderness, his longing for us to become strong and happy, his desire for our love, are all expressed over and over in Scripture, but until then I had never fully appreciated the imagery. This is the God who longs to take us up in his arms:

When Israel was a child, I loved him,
and I called my son out of Egypt ...
Yet it was I who taught Ephraim to walk,
I took them up in my arms
... I led them with cords of human kindness,
with bonds of love.
I was to them like those who lift infants to their cheeks.
(Hos 11:1-3)

In the closing chapter of Isaiah, foretelling the comfort and prosperity of the Messianic age, this imagery becomes even more pronounced:

As soon as Zion was in labour
she delivered her children.
Shall I open the womb and not deliver? ...

For thus says the Lord ...
you shall nurse and be carried on her arm,
and dandled on her knees.
As a mother comforts her child,
so I will comfort you.

As the weeks passed, and as I held our infant daughter in my arms, feeling the warmth of her downy little head and her tiny fingers with the nails I didn't dare to cut moving like small, lovely spiders over my skin, I thought the universe itself could not contain my wondering love. And when she smiled for the first time, the radiance lit my world from end to end.

FOREVER BEGINNING

Before our daughter was born I subscribed to the belief that 'As soon as you are born, you start to die'. A phrase from my college days haunted me; in Samuel Beckett's dark vision we are born 'astride of a grave. The light gleams an instant, then it's night once more'.[7] It is a sentiment as old as Ecclesiastes: 'All go to one place; all are from the dust, and all turn to dust again.' (3:20)

On that night in Bethlehem, God became our travelling companion on life's journey. He took on our human condition, and became subject to illness, to aging and to death.

Before the birth of our baby, I was conscious of time passing rapidly. As I listened with closer and closer attention to the Advent liturgies, one (from Tuesday of the second week in Advent) captured this feeling perfectly. It was Isaiah's reflection on 'all flesh is grass', recalling Psalm 103:15-16:

> As for man, his days are like grass;
> he flourishes like a flower of the field;
> for the wind passes over it, and it is gone,
> and its place knows it no more.

I didn't realise how completely my views were to change. After the miracle of our baby's arrival, I realised that birth is only a stage in becoming. Every day brought a change in her. Every day she became more of an individual. It is a process that will go on until the day she dies.

As our daughter grew and changed, I came to understand that I, too, was growing and changing. I came to see that all our life is a 'becoming'. God's work of creation does not stop with our physical birth – it is ongoing in us. Parts of us have to die in order that we may keep 'becoming'. In our bodies, millions of cells die and millions of cells are produced every second. Equilibrium has to be maintained between cell growth and cell destruction; if this equilibrium is disturbed, the consequences are potentially fatal. If cells grow faster than they die, tumours develop. If the reverse is the case, the body's ability to fight infectious diseases is either compromised or entirely absent. We must leave something behind if we are to keep growing.

BORN AGAIN, AND AGAIN

The constant 'becoming' is a spiritual one also. 'Truly, truly I say to you, unless one is born anew, he cannot enter the Kingdom of God', Christ tells us in John 3:8.[8] The experience of physical birth tells us a lot about spiritual rebirth – it is strenuous, painful and richly rewarding. When we are born, we move from darkness into light, from close confinement into the open world. We learn to breathe on our own. While the idea of the necessity for transformation permeates the New Testament, the only time Jesus uses the actual phrase 'born anew' is in his conversation with the Pharisee, Nicodemus. A cautious man, he was nervous about being seen with Jesus and so – as related in John's gospel –he 'came to Jesus by night' (Jn 3:2).

The symbolism is powerful – Nicodemus is spiritually as well as physically in the dark. Christ's words ignite a slow burning wick which will blaze into light at the most unlikely time. After the Crucifixion, when everything seemed over, Nicodemus declared himself – coming to the garden tomb bearing myrrh and aloes 'about a hundred pounds weight'.

Nicodemus, in true Pharisaic fashion, takes Jesus literally. He asks, 'How can a man be born when he is old? Can he enter a second time into his mother's womb and be born?' Jesus responds:

> Truly, truly I say to you, unless one is born of water and the Spirit, he cannot enter the Kingdom of God. That which is born of the flesh is flesh, and that which is born of the Spirit is spirit. Do not marvel that I say to you, 'You must be born anew'. The wind blows where it wills, and you hear the sound of it, but you do not know whence it comes or whither it goes; so it is with every one who is born of the Spirit. (Jn 3:5-6)[9]

We do not decide to be born. We cannot force our own birth. It is only after we receive life that our will comes into play. Nor can we force our rebirth in the Spirit. However, that rebirth is *offered* all our life. In an era where action is king we must learn to receive – and receiving can be a most difficult activity.

We can, of course, refuse spiritual rebirth. We can refuse the pain of continual death and resurrection, the daily dying and rising with Christ, the daily letting go and taking on. We can concentrate on developing our body and our intellect; we can focus on what we can see and hear and touch. We can grow from babyhood to self-consciousness without ever allowing ourselves to experience God's inner presence. We can live astride a grave.

Without life, our bodies decay; skin, muscle and tissue fall away, leaving dry bones. Without spiritual life, we are utterly perishable. We age and deteriorate with our bodies. But the breath of life which animated us at our conception is there to animate our whole being, soul as well as body.

'Can these dry bones live?' asks God in Ezekiel's ghastly vision of the Valley of Dry Bones. It is a question still addressed to us two-and-a-half thousand years later. The answer has not changed either:

> Then he said to me, 'Prophesy to these bones and say to them, O dry bones, hear the Word of the Lord. Thus says the Lord God to these bones: I will cause breath to enter you, and you shall live. I will lay sinews on you, and will cause flesh to come upon you, and cover you with skin, and put breath in you, and you shall live, and you shall know that I am the Lord.'
>
> So I prophesied as I had been commanded, and as I prophesised, suddenly there was a noise, a rattling, and the bones came together, bone to its bone. I looked, and there were sinews on them, and flesh had come upon them, and skin had covered them: but there was no breath in them. Then the Spirit said to me, 'Prophesy to the breath, prophesy mortal, and say to the breath: Thus says the Lord God: Come from the four winds, O breath, and breathe upon these slain, that they may live.'
>
> I prophesised as the Spirit commanded and breath came into them, and they lived, and stood on their feet, a vast multitude.
>
> Then he said to me, 'Mortal, these bones are the whole House of Israel. Behold, they say, "Our bones are dried up, and our hope is lost, we are cut off completely".'
>
> Therefore prophesy and say to them, Thus says the Lord God: I am going to open your graves, and bring you up from your graves, O my people, and I will bring you back to the land of Israel ... I will put my Spirit within you, and

you shall live, and I will place you on your own soil, then
you shall know that I, the Lord, have spoken and will act.
(Ezek 37:4-14)

COLLABORATORS IN CREATION

The fourteenth-century Dominican theologian and mystic,
Meister Eckhart, describes transformation and spiritual rebirth
as a continuous event: 'I would have you know that the eternal
Word is being born within the soul, its very self, no less,
unceasingly.'[10] He uses the adjective 'novissimus' to describe God
– God, according to him, is the newest and youngest thing in
the universe, exuberantly creative. According to Meister
Eckhart, the Son of God is being born unceasingly: 'If God
stopped saying his Word, but for an instant even, heaven and
earth would disappear.'[11] That Word of God is spoken in our
soul; when we stop to listen to it we are in touch with the source
of all creation. When we think the Word is not there, the reality
is that it is we who are not available to the Word. In Meister
Eckhart's blunt language:

> God is with us in our inmost soul, provided he
> finds us within and not gone out on business
> with our five senses. The soul must stop at
> home in her innermost, purest self; be ever
> within and not flying out: there God is present,
> God is nigh.[12]

In the created world, and in our own souls, the Eternal Word is
constantly coming from and returning to the Father. We

participate in that ongoing creation. We are, in the words of Teilhard de Chardin, collaborators in the creation of the universe. As such, we participate in a work which transcends our individual achievement – the completion of Creation:

> *[Man] makes his own soul* throughout all his earthly days; and at the same time he collaborates in another work ... which infinitely transcends the perspectives of his individual achievement: the completing of the world. For in presenting the Christian doctrine of salvation, it must not be forgotten that the world, too ... undergoes a sort of vast 'ontogenesis' (a vast becoming what it is) in which the development of each soul, assisted by the perceptible realities on which it depends, is but a diminished harmonic. Beneath our efforts to put spiritual form into our own lives, the world slowly accumulates, starting with the whole of matter, that which will make of it the Heavenly Jerusalem or the New Earth.[13]

In this astonishing adventure we never age. 'Know then,' says Meister Eckhart, 'that my soul is as young as when I was created, aye, much younger. And I tell you, I should be ashamed were she not younger to-morrow than to-day.'[14]

'How can a man be born when he is old?' asked Nicodemus. Christ's reply shows that age is meaningless: 'The wind blows where it chooses, and you hear the sound of it, but you do not know where it comes from or where it goes. So it is with everyone who is born of the Spirit.' (Jn 3:8)

The flicker of life that I saw leap into flame in our baby daughter is the same that Eve saw in Cain and Mary in Christ. Miraculous as it is, it pales beside the transcendent centre of energy that blazes in our souls and the knowledge that – as Meister Eckhart says – one might live a thousand years and go on growing all the time in love, just as fire will burn so long as there is wood. The bigger the fire and the stronger the wind, the more fiercely it burns. If the fire is love, and the wind is the Holy Spirit, then the time will come when the immensity of the Divine Word will be born within us unceasingly.

Giving birth is as unstoppable a process as death will be. But then, death is only another birth. The atoms in my physical body were forged in the furnaces of the stars. When my body dies, the atoms will disassemble and move on to another use. They will be endlessly recycled as long as the universe is in existence. I am in the created universe, and the created universe is in me.

God breathes eternity into my dry bones and his Word is spoken unceasingly in my soul. There is never an instant when he is not within me. With him, I make my own soul every day of my life on earth. I need have no fear of birth or rebirth, change or life or death. Instead I see them for what they are – thrilling stages along a transcendent journey home.

Notes

1   Allen Cabaniss, 'A Jewish Provenience of the Advent Antiphons?' *The Jewish Quarterly Review*, Vol. 66, No. 1 (July, 1975), pp. 39–56.

2   Ibid.

3   1 Cor 16:22.

4   St Ephraem, Deacon of Syria, 'De B. M. Virgine, Hymnus 2', taken from T.J. Lamy, *S. Ephraem Syri humni et Sermons,* Mechlin, 1882–1902, p. 526.

5   St Justin, *Dialogue with Trypho,* Chapter 100, from CCEL Online Library of the Early Church Fathers, accessed at: www.ccel.org/fathers.

6   St Irenaeus, *Against Heresies,* Book 5, Chapter 19, ibid.

7   Samuel Beckett, *Waiting for Godot,* London, Faber and Faber, 1998, p. 103.

8   From the *Revised Standard Version Bible* (RSV).

9   RSV.

10   Meister Eckhart, *Sermon XVII: In principio erat Verbum,* originally in Franz Pfeiffer, *Meister Eckhart,* translated by C. Evans, Whitefish, MT., Kessinger Publications, 1924, accessed at: www.geocities.com/ Athens/Acropolis/ 5164/eckhart.htm.

11   Ibid., *Sermon XXVI: The Feast of the Virgin.*

12   Ibid., *Sermon XXVII: Rejoice in the Lord.*

13   Pierre Teilhard de Chardin, *The Divine Milieu,* London, Fontana, 1970, p. 61.

14   Meister Eckhart, *Sermon LXXX: There is one power in the soul,* ibid.

2

INTO THE WILDERNESS

ABRAHAM, MOSES AND CHRIST

And look, you were within me and I was outside, and
there I sought you!

St Augustine, *Confessions*

'IF YOU DON'T KNOW WHERE YOU ARE, YOU DON'T KNOW WHO
YOU ARE'

The wilderness is an inescapable presence in the Old and New
Testaments, permeating them as vividly as do any of the biblical
characters. It is always there, its vastness and barrenness a stone's
throw from the habitable world. 'Wilderness' in the Bible refers
mainly to two distinct locations: the Sinai Desert, where the
Hebrews wandered for forty years after the exodus from Egypt,
and the relatively bare, uncultivated area in the south of the
Promised Land known as the Negeb, or Judean Desert.

The desert is a place of contradictions – stark, barren and
terrifying. 'The great and terrible wilderness' (Deut 8:15) is both
a place of trial and of deliverance, of purgation and illumination.
Abraham passed through the desert at least twice on his
immense migratory journey. This is the place where the
wanderings of Moses and his people culminated in the birth of

Israel as a nation; here David found refuge from Saul; here the Essenes escaped Hellenistic domination of Jerusalem; here the Zealots made their final, desperate last stand at Masada against the might of Rome; and here John the Baptist prepared for his mission. In the desert Elijah, deeply discouraged, longed for death – but it was here that God came to him in a still, small voice. This is the place where the original scapegoat was sent (Lev 16:10), carrying the sins of the people on his back; and it was to the desert that Jesus – who carried all our sins – was driven by the Spirit.

The word 'desert' conjures up vast expanses of sand stretching to the horizon. However, the desert regions of Israel are quite different, consisting of cliffs and canyons, limestone, chalk and sandstone escarpments, blinding white in the heat of the day, but where sunrise and sunset draw to the surface unimagined depths and varieties of burnished gold, singing reds and glowing pink. Huge striations on the rock face ripple like seas of stone to the arid floor in a scene of majestic lifelessness.

Standing in this splendid desolation there must be a sense of smallness against vastness, the creature a pinprick in a creation 'whose centre is everywhere, whose circumference nowhere'.[1] In the twenty-first century we have lost our sense of place. Speed of communications has made the world contract. We move vast distances for work, for pleasure. For many of us, our lifestyle is almost nomadic – we move where our employment or our inclinations take us. Familiar with many places, we are rooted in none. Where we live is where our work is, or where our relationships bring us. The technology available to us means we are always 'connected' with elsewhere – regardless of distance or time zones. Yet, however familiar we may be with the world, we are somehow not at home in it; however much we move across its surface, we no longer seem to put down roots. As the philosopher Ivan Illich puts it, 'most of the time we find ourselves out of touch with our world, out of sight of those for whom we work, out of tune with what we feel'.[2]

We are no longer connected with a place where we were born and grew up, in the way that our ancestors were. The early Irish literary tradition includes a group of writings called *dinnseanchas*, the 'poetry of place names'. The poet, or *dinnseanchai*, was in modern terminology a topographer – but the poems went far beyond describing a particular topographical feature; they related the historical and the spiritual significance of the place. People and communities were at one with the natural environment. In the words of Seamus Heaney, our sense of place 'was once more or less sacred. The landscape was sacramental, instinct with signs, implying a system of reality beyond the visible realities'.[3]

Now, we are displaced. The American writer and conservationist, Wendell Berry, famously said, 'If you don't know where you are, you don't know who you are'. In the western world, we no longer necessarily contribute to, and draw from, a particular locality (a classic example is the phenomenon of the 'dormitory town' – a place from which people commute to work, returning only to eat and sleep). Globalised goods and services have replaced the need to grow our own food, to build our own houses, to make our own entertainment. We no longer have the power to shape or satisfy our own needs. Instead of creating, we consume. Our needs are increasingly created by market forces. We are educated primarily in order to earn, and we earn primarily in order to consume. In our prime, time is there to be 'filled' and made to pass as quickly as possible; in our later years it runs through our fingers like sand – try as we may to slow it down. In a world where so much is now charted and signposted, mapped and measured, we have lost an overall sense of direction.

THE WILDERNESS WITHIN

Where, in all this hurly burly, do we find a holy place, a place where we can be apart and encounter God? One of Christ's paradoxical sayings is that we have to lose our life to save it. Equally, we have to go where there are no paths in order to find our direction.

The wilderness, or desert, is the ultimate trackless zone. In the Bible it is – again paradoxically – a place of transformation and revelation. This 'howling waste' (Deut 32:10), infested with serpents and scorpions (Deut 8:15), swept by deadly winds (Is 21:1; Jer 4:11) is at the same time a holy place, where the glory of God descended upon Moses 'like a devouring fire' (Ex 24:17).

Passage through the wilderness was an integral part of their mission for Abraham, Moses, Elijah, John and Jesus. But where is such a place to be found in a modern suburban life? In our frenetic, noisy, peopled world, where are we to find these great stark tracts of silence and isolation, these testing grounds with their lurking dangers of heat and thirst and wild beasts? Where are we to find a place where we strip away everything that is superfluous, everything that distracts us or deadens us, and place ourselves utterly in God's hands?

To find the answer, I retraced the desert journey – sometimes with Abraham, Moses, Elijah and John, but especially with Jesus, since it is above all in his life that we seek the meaning of our own. The more I read the biblical accounts, the clearer it became that the journey is metaphorical as well as literal. The wilderness exists on maps, but it also exists within us.

For many of us, our 'selves' are like haunted houses – tenanted with the ghosts of past loves and losses, triumphs and disappointments, achievements and failures. Sorrows and rage as old as infancy can lurk within us and the accumulation of a lifetime's shortcomings can make our 'selves' uncomfortable and unwelcoming places in which to be, so that we try to spend as much time as possible outside ourselves. We fill our days with noise and activity; sometimes we deaden our pain with alcohol, food, work, sex or drugs. An Episcopal monk and spiritual writer, Martin L. Smith, describes our habitual condition as one of being under an anaesthetic:

> Most of us have a primary defence mechanism against being overwhelmed by the pain of the world and our own pain. It is as if we administer to ourselves an anaesthetic to numb its impact. The price we pay is that it also numbs our capacity for joy, but until we surrender to the Spirit of God we reckon the price to be worth it.[4]

If we don't confront the wilderness inside, we can never overcome our own isolation. If we don't sufficiently accept and love ourselves, we can never really enter into communion with others and with God. Was this what St Augustine was getting at when he cried, 'And look, you were within me and I was outside, and there I sought for you'?[5]

It is almost never too late to make this journey, although the longer we leave it the harder it becomes. Our distractions, addictions or avoidances grow like tumours around vital organs. If we leave the tumours untreated, we die. The longer we wait to remove them, the more potentially deadly the operation.

Extreme youth or extreme age does not excuse us from making the journey into the wilderness. John the Baptist appears to have entered the desert at a very young age, in preparation for his mission as the Forerunner. Abraham – then known as Abram – was seventy-five years old when he received that irresistible call, 'Go forth from your country and your kindred and your father's house to the land that I will show you' (Gen 12:1).

'So Abram went'. He left Haran in southern Mesopotamia (now in modern Turkey) and travelled south-west across Syria and through Damascus. He probably followed the ancient trading route known as the 'King's Highway' from Damascus along the hilly backbone of Jordan and into Canaan. He crossed though Shechem (today the Palestinian town of Nablus) and Bethel; then south to the Negev desert where famine forced him south-west to Egypt and the fertile Nile Delta. After a sojourn in Egypt he retraced his steps through the Negev to Canaan, eventually dying at Hebron.

The immense journey marked out a great triangle which roughly defines the area of the Promised Land and was Abraham's response to God's command to 'walk through the length and breadth of the land, for I will give it to you' (Gen 13:17). In the course of the journey, his long abandoned hopes of a child by Sarah, his wife, were realised, and he became 'the ancestor of a multitude of nations' (Gen 17:5), the spiritual father of the world's Christians, Jews and Muslims – half of the people alive on earth today. And all this was initiated at a time in his life when he might have reasonably been looking forward to a tranquil old age! There is another dimension to Abraham's journey. Pope John Paul II, in a homily given on Wednesday, 23 February 2000, asked:

> Are we talking about the route taken by one of the many migrations typical of an era when sheep-rearing was a basic form of economic life? Probably. Surely though, *it was not only this.* In Abraham's life, which marks the beginning of salvation history, we can already perceive another meaning of the call and the promise. The land to which human beings, guided by the voice of God, are moving, *does not belong exclusively to the geography of this world.* Abraham, the believer who accepts God's invitation, is someone heading towards a promised land that is not of this world.[6]

The journey of Moses took forty years. It seems to have been a much more tedious journey than that of Abraham, and it is very easy to empathise with Moses' often discontented travelling companions. The Hebrews left Egypt in a blaze of glory. Their years under a cruel oppressor ended with the first Passover, and they crossed the Red Sea on dry land. Their 'song of the sea' in Exodus 15 rings with joy and confidence in a delivering God.

But by the time the Hebrews reached the Wilderness of Sin, they had had enough of desert privations. They wanted to return to slavery in Egypt, saying bitterly to Moses and Aaron:

> If only we had died by the hand of the Lord in the land of Egypt, when we sat by the fleshpots and ate our fill of bread, for you have brought us out to this wilderness to kill this whole assembly with hunger. (Ex 16:3)

The miseries of slavery had been forgotten. The past was now viewed selectively, and seemed a lot safer and more secure. In contrast, the future they faced with Moses was unknown and comfortless. The Hebrews wanted to reverse their journey.

As I have often done. I have dabbled in the wilderness and then rushed back to the known comfort zones of my own Egypt. How often have I started Lent, for example, with a determination to advance on my journey! How often have I resolutely put behind me the many obstacles to my spiritual progress only to lose heart at the first hurdle! Like Pharaoh's chariots, my wheels were clogged 'so that they turned with difficulty' (Ex 14:25). When the vastness of the wilderness opened up before me, slavery suddenly seemed a lot more attractive.

Despite their yearnings for Egypt's 'fleshpots', in Exodus 17:1 we read 'From the Wilderness of Sin the whole congregation of the Israelites journeyed by stages, as the Lord commanded'. There is no standing still – God asks us to keep moving. As the Hebrews did – but in the next breath we are told that they began to complain again. There was no water to drink, so they asked Moses, 'Why did you bring us out of Egypt, to kill us and our children and livestock with thirst ... Is the Lord among us or not?' (Ex 17:3, 7). Again the Lord provides, but by the time they reach Rephidim the Hebrews are 'quarrelling' again. So it goes on throughout the Exodus journey – a rollercoaster of ups and downs, of enthusiasm and grumbling, of devotion to God, and worshipping a golden calf. Amid all this, we have the giving of the Ten Commandments, the Ark of the Covenant, the revelation of God's name and the renewal of God's covenant with his people.

Even within sight of the Promised Land, the people lost heart. The spies they sent to reconnoitre the land came back with reports of a gigantic and powerful people – 'to ourselves we seemed like grasshoppers, and so we seemed to them' (Num 13:33). The old refrain went up:

> Would that we had died in the land of Egypt! Or that we had died in this wilderness! Why is the Lord bringing us into this land to fall by the sword? Our wives and our little ones will become booty; would it not be better for us to go back to Egypt? (Num 14:2-3)

Only Caleb and Joshua remonstrated with the people. In anger, God prolonged the sojourn in the wilderness so that none of those alive at that time, with the exception of Caleb and Joshua, would cross into Canaan.

PASSAGE AND PURIFICATION

The forty years wandering seem pointless until one realises what was achieved in that time. The people Moses led out of Egypt had been enslaved for four centuries. The Hebrew tribes of Israel entered Egypt voluntarily, probably about 1600 BC, at the invitation of Jacob's son Joseph, then a high official in Pharaoh's administration. They initially prospered, and their numbers multiplied over three centuries. However, 'there arose a new king over Egypt, who did not know Joseph' (Ex 1:8). Under his rule, Hebrews were disenfranchised and forced into slave labour in Egypt's massive building programme and in the noxious conditions of the turquoise mines. Their spirit was utterly broken by centuries of bondage. The mixed multitude which set out from Egypt was in no condition to take possession of the land promised to it. In the wilderness years, Moses brought God's law to the people and welded them together in disciplined monotheism.

These stiff-necked and vacillating people have been a source of immense encouragement to me; however often they stumbled and longed to turn back, they nonetheless kept moving – urged relentlessly forward by God. They must have longed to spend more time at each oasis, especially at the large oasis of Kadesh Barnea between the deserts of Sin, Shur and Paran where they camped for many years. But in their subsequent wanderings the Hebrews were transformed. The discontented mob became a great nation and the covenant made with Abraham was fulfilled. The biblical desert is a place of passage and purification. In the desert landscapes of our souls we must learn that God is with us at every stage of the journey. He is God of the wilderness as well as God of the land flowing with milk and honey. But to reach the latter, we must cross the former. We, too, need to cast off our inertia and our false gods if we are to enter into the Promised Land.

When John the Baptist emerged from the wilderness to baptise Jesus, we are told by Mark that Jesus 'saw the heavens torn apart and the Spirit as a dove descending like a dove on him'. The same verb is used by Mark (15:38) to describe how the curtain in the Holy of Holies is rent in two at the moment that Christ's own torn body died on Calvary. The phrase is made even more powerful by the fact that it is used in the present passive – literally, 'the heavens *were being* rent asunder'. How extraordinary to realise that they are still being rent apart for our own baptism and for every baptism!

A voice sounds from the heavens: 'You are my Son, the Beloved; with you I am well pleased.' Immediately after this, Matthew and Luke tell us that Jesus was 'led' by the Spirit into the wilderness. Mark, however, puts it much more strongly: 'the Spirit immediately drove him out into the wilderness.' It so often happens that after an experience of great closeness to God, we are put to the test. Dejection can follow hard on the heels of exhilaration. We are never more open to temptation than when we feel spiritually strong. We can run out of spiritual steam as quickly as the Hebrews regretted the leaving of Egypt.

The first Adam was tempted in a garden; the new Adam was tempted in a desert with very different results. The verb 'to tempt' can also – and perhaps more accurately – be translated 'to test'. The original Hebrew word is often used in the context of testing the genuineness of coins. The durability of metal has to be tested before it is used; if we are to be used by God, our strength must also be tested.

In his book *Foundations for Centering Prayer,* the Cistercian writer Thomas Keating sees Jesus in the desert as the representative of the human race:

> He bears within himself the experience of the
> human predicament in its raw intensity. Hence,
> he is vulnerable to the temptations of Satan. ...
> The temptations of Satan are allowed by God to
> help us confront our own evil tendencies. If
> relatives and friends fail to bring out the worst
> in us, Satan is always around to finish the job.
> Self-knowledge is experiential; it tastes the full
> depths of human weakness.[7]

The wilderness inside us is a place of testing, where the power of false gods is broken. It is a place of encounter with ourselves, with our inner demons and with God. To enter it, we have to leave behind all our elaborately constructed avoidance techniques. We have to enter naked, silent and alone, without food or drink, sex, drugs or deadlines, safety nets or empty spiritual practices. Only through making ourselves vulnerable to our own pain and fear can we make ourselves open to the experience of loving and of being loved. Like the Hebrews leaving Egypt, we have to ease off the shackles of slavery to false gods. The false gods are different for each of us – a desire for money, status or power, an addiction, an old resentment or hatred, an extramarital love affair, an obsession with work, a refusal to advance on our journey for fear that we may not be able to complete it – but all have this in common: the false gods displace the real God for us. They drain our energies and our hope. Life with them has no flavour; life without them is unimaginable – a wilderness too huge and bare to contemplate. We have become so accustomed to our enslavement that our chains have grown comfortable. We sit by our 'fleshpots'; we 'eat our bread to the full'. We shrink before the colossal aridity of the desert.

No short cuts to the Promised Land

Even Jesus had to be 'driven' into the wilderness. Just as he shared our human nature, our birth and growing pains, our loves and terrors, he allowed himself to be tested as we all must be tested. If what is tested in us is our weakest point, then the temptation of Jesus seems to centre on his feelings about his mission. Twice Satan says, 'If you are the Son of God ...' Does this suggest that Jesus himself is not certain about who he is? It is easy to empathise with him if this is so. It is easy to feel disbelief in our own worth and destiny. It is so easy to deny the colossal reality that we are living temples, in which the Word of God is eternally spoken. The wild beasts of Christ's wilderness haunt our internal landscapes too – beasts of terror, rage and despair. So we turn to Jesus and see how he coped.

'If you are the Son of God, command these stones to become bread', the devil said. Christ's reply, 'One does not live by bread alone' (Mt 4:4), is a direct quotation from Moses in the wilderness, addressing his vacillating followers (Deut 8:3). It speaks just as directly to us today – we can starve in the desert of our souls without the word of God to feed us.

Satan, bringing Jesus to the pinnacle, invites him to test whether he is, indeed, the One the psalmist wrote about: 'He will give his angels charge of you, to guard you in all your ways. On their hands they will bear you up, so that you will not dash your foot against a stone.' (Ps 91:11-12) Again, Jesus quotes Moses: 'Do not put the Lord your God to the test.' (Deut 6:16)

The striking parallels which Christ draws between his forty days in the desert and the Israelites' forty years in the wilderness are full of significance. Jesus emphasises our dependence on God, and our inability to accelerate our passage to the Promised Land. Satan was offering a quick fix to any doubts Jesus may have had, and Jesus turned it down. There are no short cuts on our journey. The Promised Land was not a forty-year journey from Egypt, but forty years was what it took to prepare the Israelites to take possession of the Promised Land.

In recalling the experience of the forty years of wandering, there is another subtext. The Israelites faced a massive recurring temptation which we, too, encounter: the desire to say 'enough – we've tried this and it isn't working. Let's turn back'. But they found that God is Lord of the desert as well as Lord of the oasis. The only way we can know that is to experience it. It may be a long and a hard journey to the Promised Land, but the only way to get to it is through the wilderness. The alternative is to stagnate in our own particular Egypt. If we do that, we will never experience transformation in, and transformation *of* the desert. By saying, 'I can't go any further' we will be the earthen vessels striving with the potter; 'does the clay say to the one who fashions it, "What are you making?" or "Your work has no handles"?' (Is 45:9)

The Promised Land is waiting for us to start the journey towards it – not tomorrow, not in some faraway time when we will have dispensed with all the things that now distract us or anaesthetise us, but *now*. As God said to Moses on the hills of Moab, within sight of the Promised Land:

> This commandment that I am commanding you today
> is not too hard for you, neither is it too far away. It is not

in heaven, that you should say, 'Who will go up for us to heaven, and get it for us so that we may hear and observe it?' Neither is it beyond the sea, that you should say, 'Who will cross to the other side of the sea for us, and get it for us so that we may hear and observe it?' No; the word is very near to you; it is in your mouth and in your heart for you to observe. (Deut 30:14)

If we have the courage to place ourselves in the hands of our Maker, we will feel the heavens open and rain grace down upon us, transforming our desert:

> The wilderness and the dry land shall be glad,
> the desert shall rejoice and blossom;
> like the crocus it shall blossom abundantly,
> and rejoice with joy and singing. (Is 35:1)

We will hear the words of Moses to the Israelites as they emerge from the wilderness and understand that: 'The eternal God is your refuge, and underneath are the everlasting arms' (Deut 33:27).[8] We will know that angels have ministered to us without our realising it. And, because Christ went through the same experience, we will be able to take comfort in the knowledge that he is both the Way and the Wayfarer.

Notes

1   Blaise Pascal, *Pensées*, Penguin Classics, 1995, p. 60.

2   Ivan Illich, *The Right to Useful Unemployment*, London, Marion Boyars Publishers Ltd., 1996, p. 11.

3   Seamus Heaney, *Preoccupations*, London, Faber & Faber, 1984, p. 131.

4   Martin L. Smith, *A Season for the Spirit,* London, Fount 1991, p. 21

5   St Augustine, *Confessions,* Book 10, Chapter 27, Signet Classics, 2001, p. 279.

6   Homily on 'The Commemoration of Abraham' given by Pope John Paul II on Wednesday, 23 February 2000, accessed at: www.catholicculture.org.

7   Thomas Keating, *Foundations for Centering Prayer and the Christian Contemplative Life,* New York, Continuum, 2002, p. 288.

8   RSV; this verse is omitted from the *New Revised Standard Version* (NRSV).

3

THE RELUCTANT PROPHET
Jonah and the Comfort Zone

It is a fearful thing to fall into the hands of the living
God.
But it is a much more fearful thing to fall out of them.

D.H. Lawrence, 'The Hands of God'

The most unexpected book in the Bible

I discovered Jonah and Pinocchio at about the same time, when
I was six or seven years old. The Pinocchio I encountered was
not the Disney version, but a battered copy of Carlo Collodi's
original book with Attilio Mussino's haunting illustrations. Of
all the episodes in the story the one which made the greatest
impact on me was the scene where Pinocchio the marionette is
swallowed by the Terrible Shark. I read and reread with
horrified fascination the descriptions of the shark's belly – 'two
miles long, not counting the tail'. It was the stuff of nightmares
to a child who was terrified of the dark:

> Around him all was darkness, a darkness so deep and so
> black that for a moment he thought he had put his head
> into an inkwell. He listened for a few moments and

heard nothing. Once in a while a cold wind blew on his face. At first he could not understand where that wind was coming from, but after a while he understood that it came from the lungs of the monster.[1]

Pinocchio sees a faint light in the distance and splashes his way toward it through thick, oily water which stinks of fish. He discovers his creator Gepetto, who has been living in the fish's belly for two years, 'a little old man, white as snow'. The accompanying drawing of Gepetto with his great white beard had a vaguely biblical feel to it. The errant puppet throws himself into his maker's arms and together they escape the yawning darkness.

It is not surprising that the stories of Pinocchio and Jonah became tightly interwoven in my child's mind. There were many similarities: both protagonists were swallowed by a fish and each encountered his maker before escaping. One story seemed no more fanciful than the other. Over the years my perception of Jonah remained childlike; all I recalled of him was the sojourn in the fish's stomach, etched forever in my mind in the chiaroscuro of Mussino's illustrations. Jonah seemed as much a creature of fable as Pinocchio.

I am sure I am not alone in associating Jonah with the whale, and only with the whale. The big fish which swallows Jonah seems to swallow the whole book of Jonah as well. Nothing prepared me for the surprises I found when I revisited it in recent years. This is a jewel of a book – vivid, unexpected, funny, dramatic and touchingly human. Above all, here is a prophet with whom one can identity far more easily than with his loftier peers. This is no Elijah, no Isaiah – rather a cantankerous, self-absorbed, stubborn individual, impatient with others and knowing better than God what is good for him. His short book is located among the 'Minor Prophets'[2] of the Old Testament. It follows the unremittingly gloomy book of Obadiah and precedes the only slightly less doom-laden book of Micah. Properly speaking, the book of Jonah is not a prophecy at all, even though Jonah was a prophet. The only prophecy in the book is the nine-word prophecy to Nineveh, which is not fulfilled.

This is only the beginning of the unusual aspects of the book of Jonah. All the other books of the Minor Prophets are collections of the prophecies of the individual prophet; Jonah's is the only book to tell the prophet's own story. And he tells it mainly in straight narrative rather than in poetry or prophetic prose.

Jonah is the only Minor Prophet whose mission takes place on foreign soil and to Gentiles. He is the only one of the Minor Prophets to be mentioned by Jesus (Mt 12:40, 16:4; Lk 11:30, 32). He is the only prophet to begin by refusing his mission. The opening three verses stopped me dead in my tracks:

> Now the word of the Lord came to Jonah the son of Amittai, saying 'Go at once to Nineveh, that great city, and cry out against it; for their wickedness has come up before me'. But Jonah set out to flee to Tarshish from the presence of the Lord. He went down to Joppa and found a ship going to Tarshish; so he paid the fare and went on board, to go with them to Tarshish, away from the presence of the Lord.

Jonah did not do things by half measures. The repeated mention of Tarshish is significant. Tarshish is believed to have been in south-western Spain – the farthest westerly harbour for the ancient world's greatest seafarers, the Phoenicians. It was about as far from Nineveh as anyone could get. How easy it is to get a boat going in the wrong direction!

This arresting beginning made me feel that there was a lot more to the book of Jonah than the whale. And so it turned out, as I set off on the most bizarre journey of the Old Testament.

THE IMPOSSIBLE MISSION

It begins in Galilee, where Jonah lived at Gath-hepher, four miles from Nazareth, eight centuries before the coming of Christ. He was a prophet of note during the reign of King Jeroboam II and correctly foretold the expansion of Israel's borders under that forceful leader (2 Kings 14:25). Jeroboam was the most powerful king of Israel's northern kingdom since King Ahab, Elijah's arch-enemy, sixty-two years earlier. The years preceding Jeroboam's ascent to the throne had been difficult ones. The Arameans of Damascus had become a major force in the region, capturing many territories from Israel. Further north, the Assyrians were gathering strength, conquering much of the Middle East from the tenth to the seventh centuries BC. They implemented a ruthless strategy of mass deportation among defeated nations, moving tens of thousands of people across their empire. Israel had already prostrated itself before Assyria; the earliest known picture of an Israelite appears on one of the panels of the Black Obelisk at the British Museum, excavated twenty miles south of Nineveh. Erected in 835 BC, it depicts Jeroboam's great-grandfather Jehu kneeling before the Assyrian King Shalmaneser III. The panel below the picture reads: 'The tribute of Jehu, son of Omri: I received from him silver, gold, a golden bowl, a golden vase with painted bottoms, golden tumblers, gold buckets, tin, a staff for a King [and] spears.'

Israel's borders had been steadily contracting, and alliances shifted like quicksand in a part of the world which was as volatile then as it is now. War followed war. During Jeroboam's reign, the Assyrians withdrew temporarily to address problems on their domestic front, striking a crippling blow at Damascus as they left. Jeroboam was quick to take advantage of the resulting power vacuum; he recovered the territories of Israel which had been lost to Damascus and he restored the boundaries which marked the empire of King David, when Israel's territorial control had been at its greatest.

The lull during the reign of Jeroboam was short-lived. Not many years after Jonah died, the Assyrians utterly destroyed Israel's northern kingdom. The ten northern tribes were transported vast distances and dispersed, becoming utterly lost to recorded history. The southern two-tribe kingdom of Judah survived, only to be conquered in 587 BC by Nebuchadnezzar. (It was at this point that the captives became known as Jews, a name deriving from Judah.)

The Assyrians were renowned for their cruelty. Impaling, dismembering and flaying were common practice. The following excerpt from the annals of King Ashurnasirpal II, who reigned a century before Jonah's time, gives a flavour of the savagery:

> With the masses of my troops and by my furious battle onset I stormed, I captured the city; 600 of their warriors I put to the sword; 3,000 captives I burned with fire; I did not leave a single one among them alive to serve as hostage. Hulai, their governor, I captured alive. Their corpses I formed into pillars; their young men and maidens I burned in the fire. Hulai, their governor, I flayed, his skin I spread upon the wall of the city of Damdamusa; the city I destroyed, I devastated with fire.[3]

At the heart of this fearsome military state was the massive stronghold of Nineveh. It would later become the capital of the entire Assyrian empire. Today its ruins lie across the Tigris River from modern Mosul, in Iraq. The vast city walls were eight miles in circumference and had fifteen monumental gateways, all constructed with seemingly endless supplies of forced labour from defeated nations. Thousands of people lived within its walls. Its position on the northern arc of the so-called 'Fertile Crescent', and on the great trade routes linking the Mediterranean and the Indian Ocean, was central to its enormous prosperity. Imperial highways led away from Nineveh to the subjugated territories of Babylon, Egypt and Syria. The city was an important centre of worship for the warlike goddess Ishtar, depicted as 'covered with combat and arrayed with terror' – she was also the goddess of lust and fertility, and sacred prostitution was part of her cult.

'Go at once to Nineveh', said the Lord to Jonah. For Jonah, Nineveh would have symbolised all that was wicked, cruel and heathen. While the prophets Elijah and Elisha healed and worked miracles among Gentiles, Jonah is the only Old Testament prophet charged with an entire mission to Gentiles.

There was nothing to prepare him for this; the pagans, with their idolatry and foul practices, were regarded as untouchables from the dawn of the Old Testament.

Warnings against idolatry abound in the Torah, the law transmitted by God to his people though Moses in the first five books of the Bible. The sinners are condemned with the sin, 'Pour out your anger on the nations that do not know you, and on the kingdoms that do not call on your name!' exhorts the Psalmist (Ps 79:6). And again, 'Add guilt to their guilt; may they have no acquittal from you. Let them be blotted out of the book of the living' (Ps 69:27, 28). These are phrases with which Jonah would have been intimately familiar: they come from the psalms of David and Asaph. (The Psalms were written over a period of several centuries, many written after the time of Jonah. Those written by David and his priest-musician Asaph were written two centuries before the time of Jonah.)

Asking Jonah to go and warn the Ninevites was akin to asking a Jew to preach to the Nazis in the streets of Berlin during the Third Reich. It cannot have been hard for him to rationalise his refusal, with the weight of Mosaic Law behind him. We know from later events that he does not lack courage – it is outrage and not fear which motivates his resistance to God's request. Why should these monsters be spared by a single act of repentance? Why should they not be made to realise – and pay for – the gravity of their offences?

Like Jonah, I have had times of being appalled at what God seemed to be asking me to do. 'God can't mean me to do this', I told myself. 'There's no point in doing something if my heart isn't in it. I can serve God much better in a different way.' I rationalised my reaction by convincing myself that I must have misunderstood God's message – unlike Jonah, who was in no doubt about what God was asking of him. Jonah more than likely felt that his particular talents would be much better employed at home, where his own people were sorely in need of guidance under a king who – while efficient – was also corrupt. We were each missing the point.

SLEEPING THROUGH DANGER

Jonah had scarcely left land when the Lord 'hurled a great wind on the sea, and such a mighty storm came upon the sea that the ship threatened to break up'. The terrified sailors began to call on their gods. It is a measure of the extreme danger they faced that they began to offload cargo to lighten the boat. And what was Jonah doing in the midst of this tumult? 'Jonah, meanwhile, had gone down into the hold of the ship and had lain down, and was fast asleep.' The captain comes to Jonah and cries, 'What are you doing sound asleep? Get up, call on your god!'

Putting off a major task depletes our energy far more than action does. The knowledge of what we *should* be doing agitates us, no matter how hard we try to push it to the back of our mind. It lurks at the edge of our consciousness, draining the moment, devitalising the present.

The Latin Vulgate translation of the captain's words is very illuminating: *'Quid tu sopore deprimeris?'* ('why are you weighed down by sleep?') The word 'depression' has its root in this verb 'to press down'. Excessive sleeping is a frequent symptom of clinical depression. When we are in pain, in denial, we take refuge in sleep. We sleep when we have no faith, no hope. We sleep to stop the thinking. We sleep physically and metaphorically – we can sleep through extreme moral danger. When we ignore what we know we need to do we escape the storm in our minds by abdicating responsibility and retreating into numbness. Sleep is the ultimate comfort zone, the primal womb to which we return nightly for rebirth and regeneration. It is when we don't want to leave the womb that the trouble starts.

Jonah was asleep – to himself, to God, to the needs of others. He was as deaf to the call of the captain as he was to God's call. In despair, the sailors cast lots to establish on whose account the storm has come upon them. The lot fell on Jonah and they besieged him with questions: 'Tell us why this calamity has come upon us? What is your occupation? Where do you come from? What is your country? And of what people are you?'

Finally Jonah speaks. Interestingly, he doesn't answer the first question, despite the fact that his occupation, as a prophet of God, must be his pre-eminent concern at this moment. Instead he replies: 'I am a Hebrew; I worship the Lord, the God of heaven, who made the sea and the dry land.' The heathen mariners, aghast, ask Jonah what he should have been asking himself: '"What is this you have done!" For the men knew he was fleeing from the presence of the Lord, because he had told them.' Jonah tells them they will have to throw him into the raging sea, which they reluctantly do. The sea is immediately still, whereupon the pagan sailors 'feared the Lord even more, and they offered a sacrifice to the Lord and made vows'. And in this way Jonah, running away from his mission to the Gentiles of Nineveh, makes his first Gentile conversions.

You would imagine that, at this point, Jonah himself would start praying. However, he remains silent as he is thrown into the sea. He is silent as he is swallowed by the 'great fish' the Lord sends. He is silent for some time in the belly of the creature. He does not ask God to save him. It seems that where he now finds himself is better than the alternative, which is doing God's will. The womb-like associations are inescapable. Here is Jonah, in the darkness of the fish's belly, at the depths of the ocean, which is itself in ancient mythology a powerful symbol of the womb.

Finally, from this most withdrawn, hidden place he breaks his silence – not to pray for deliverance, but to sing his thanksgiving. He has realised that this entombment is not an end, but a beginning. He prays from a womb, not a tomb, and his prayer heralds rebirth.

THE GOD OF SECOND CHANCES

As a description of the hell of hiding oneself from God's presence, Jonah's psalm is unparalleled in the Bible. For anyone who has closed ears and heart to God's voice over a long period, Jonah's phrases fall like hammer blows:

> I called to the Lord, out of my distress, and he answered me;
> Out of the belly of Sheol I cried, and you heard my voice.
> You cast me into the deep, into the heart of the seas,
> And the waves surrounded me;
> All your waves and your billows passed over me.
> Then I said, 'I am cast out from your sight;
> How shall I again look upon your holy temple?'

'Belly of Sheol' is a phrase wholly Jonah's own, used nowhere else in the Bible. 'Sheol' is the abyss, the pit of destruction. This is the place from which nobody returns and where all hope ceases. In the oldest book of the Bible, Job describes it as the land 'whence I shall not return ... the land of gloom and deep darkness, the land of gloom and chaos, where light is like darkness' (Job 10:21, 22). Isaiah says 'those who go down to the Pit cannot hope for your faithfulness' (Is 38:18). Even though God is there as he is everywhere, when we go to Sheol we place ourselves beyond his ability to hear and to help us:

> Do you work wonders for the dead?
> Do the shades rise up to praise you?
> Is your steadfast love declared in the grave,
> or thy faithfulness in Abaddon [Sheol]?
> Are your wonders known in the darkness,
> or your saving help in the land of forgetfulness?
> (Ps 88:10-12)

However, Jonah, unbelievably, is coming back from the land of no return – as Christ will do eight hundred years later. In the land where God is deaf and silent, Jonah declares 'you heard my voice'. He evokes, most vividly, the extent of his descent:

> The waters closed in over me, the deep surrounded me; weeds were wrapped around my head at the roots of the mountains.
> I went down to the land whose bars closed upon me for ever;
> yet you brought up my life from the Pit, O Lord my God.

Descent and ascent. Down to Joppa, down to the bowels of the ship, down to the belly of the fish, down to the depths of the ocean. Down to Hell. And on the third day Jonah is delivered from his living tomb. The tale now turns to one of ascent as the fish vomits Jonah onto dry land and he is back where he started.

> Then the word of the Lord came to Jonah the second time, saying 'Get up, go to Nineveh, that great city, and proclaim to it the message that I tell you'. So Jonah set out and went to Nineveh.

This is the God of second chances. It is no coincidence that the book of Jonah has been read for two thousand years at the Mishnah or afternoon service of Yom Kippur, the holiest and most solemn of Jewish holidays. This feast is the culminating point of the great season of repentance which starts with Rosh Hashanah, the Jewish New Year. The ten days between Rosh Hashanah and Yom Kippur are known as the 'Days of Awe'. They are a time of introspection and repentance in which the sins of the previous year are contemplated and repented of. According to the Talmud, God opens three books on the first day of the year: one for the wicked, one for the good and the third for the large numbers who fall somewhere in between. The fate of the wicked and the good is determined on the spot; the destiny of the 'in betweens' is suspended until Yom Kippur.

Yom Kippur is the last chance to change the judgement, to demonstrate repentance and make amends before God's 'Book of Life' is closed and sealed until the following year. As Yom Kippur ends, a final service called 'Neilah' (meaning 'locked') offers a last opportunity for repentance. It is the only service of the year where the doors to the Ark (where the Torah scrolls are stored) remain open from beginning to end of the service, signifying that the gates of heaven are open at this time:

> This is the turning point of the day. We have descended into the bowels of the earth with Jonah, we have sunk to the base of the mountains, we have felt our souls fainting within us, and now we begin to feel ourselves turning. Outside, the darkness will come, the city will call us back, and the world beyond will envelop us in its complex chaos once again. We are indeed like Jonah, shrouded by the womb-like protection of a fish, ready to make this final journey back to Nineveh.[4]

And what a journey Jonah's to Nineveh was! The miracle of his survival in the whale pales in comparison with what happened next. Jonah went into the great city of Nineveh and with eight words converted the entire population. 'Forty days more, and Nineveh shall be overthrown.' It is the shortest and most effective sermon on record. 'And the people of Nineveh believed God; they proclaimed a fast and everyone, great and small, put on sackcloth.' (The Ninevites may have been prepared for Jonah's message by several catastrophes in the preceding six years. Between 765 and 759 BC Nineveh had been ravaged by famine, two plagues and a massive flood. In the middle of this disastrous period, on 15 June 763, a total eclipse of the sun occurred – a fearful omen in the ancient world.)

The king dressed himself in sackcloth and sat down in ashes. He ordered all the people and all the animals of Nineveh to fast from food and water, to wear sackcloth, to turn from their wicked ways and cry 'mightily' to God. 'Who knows,' he exclaims, 'God may relent and change his mind; he may turn from his fierce anger, so that we do not perish!'

It is hard not to smile at the image of the cattle of Nineveh clad in sackcloth and lowing mightily on command. However, the involvement of the animals in both the repentance and subsequent salvation of the city does give a sense of the extent of God's involvement with his creation. Nothing is too great or too humble for his concern and love.

ALLOWING OURSELVES TO BE USED BY GOD

Nineveh repents, God spares Nineveh and Jonah is incandescent with rage. For modern readers the fish story is difficult to assimilate; we find the mercy God showed to Nineveh easier to accept. For Jonah it was the other way around.

> Oh Lord! Is not this what I said when I was still in my own country? That is why I fled to Tarshish in the beginning; for I knew that you are a gracious God and merciful, slow to anger, and abounding in steadfast love ... And now, O Lord, please take my life from me for it is better for me to die than to live.

It was not cowardice that made Jonah flee from God's initial call. He didn't want to go to Nineveh because he knew the power of his own preaching and he dreaded the possibility that the hated Assyrians would listen to him and be spared.

To us, steeped in the cult of the individual, it is very easy to empathise with Jonah. He had an amazing talent, but he wanted to be the one to decide how best it should be used. It is as hard for us as it was for Jonah to accept that at times our roles will not be centre stage.

Instead, we can be called upon to be a conduit through which God's will is accomplished. Sometimes it doesn't matter if our hearts are not in what we do – the fact that we do it can be enough for God to achieve astonishing results though us. So it was with Jonah, the most reluctant prophet in the Bible.

In Christ's parable of the talents, the fact that the word 'talent' has a dual meaning is significant. The master in the parable gave to each according to his ability and he clearly expected his servants to use their talents productively in his service. In order to increase the amount, they had to spend it. We know from the parable that failure is not necessarily the loss of what we are given, but a lack of effort to increase it.

Jonah was greatly resistant to the idea of spending his talent in this particular way. His spiritual landscape was as circumscribed and confined as the whale's belly. While finding his own deliverance perfectly acceptable, he did not want God to extend the same generosity to people he judged as undeserving. Jonah reduced God to a tribal deity, the exclusive property of Jonah's own people. His people, and only his people, are the proper focus of God's love and attention. He tries to force God into his own small world. Was he so very different – are we so very different – from the people of Nineveh as described by the prophet Zephaniah: 'Is this the exultant city that lived secure, that said to itself, "I am and there is none else?"' (Zeph 2:15)

According to Mosaic Law, sin was cleansed through righteousness, and righteousness could only be achieved by rigid and consistent observance of the law. In this legalistic approach, the breaking of a single tenet of the law was the equivalent of breaking the entire law. The notion of deliverance from a lifetime's wickedness though a single act of repentance would have been utterly alien to Jonah. What was the point of fidelity to the Mosaic Law if one could just as easily be saved without it? Eight centuries on, Jesus will tell the parable of the vineyard owner who pays the last workers as much as the first. Those who had worked from early morning grumbled, 'These last worked only one hour, and you have made them equal to us who have borne the burden of the day and the scorching heat'. To which the vineyard owner replies, 'Am I not allowed to do what I choose with what belongs to me? Or are you envious because I am generous?' (Mt 20:12, 15).

Jonah certainly begrudged God's generosity in this instance. He went and sat outside the city, waiting to see what would become of it. Clearly, he hoped God would reconsider his decision to save it. Again, one can identify with him. Few of us are completely immune from *schadenfreude.*

God, ever patient, causes a plant to grow up and shade Jonah from the scorching heat. Always willing to take, if not to give, Jonah was 'very happy'. But when dawn came up the next day, God sent a worm to destroy the plant and, to make matters worse, appointed 'a sultry east wind, and the sun beat down upon this head of Jonah so that he was faint; and he asked that he might die, and said "It is better for me to die than to live"'.

Luther describes Jonah beautifully:

> This is, I think, a queer and odd saint who is angry
> because of God's mercy for sinners ... He does not even
> change when God punishes him for his unreasonable
> anger ... and yet he is God's dear child. He chats so
> uninhibitedly with God as though he were not in the
> least afraid of him, as indeed he is not; he confides in
> him as a father.[5]

Perhaps this is the secret of God's patience with Jonah. Stiff-necked and curmudgeonly as he is, Jonah is nonetheless honest and courageous, unafraid to enter into a real dialogue with God. He is obedient in action but does not attempt to pretend that he is compliant in his heart. He is completely true to himself.

CAGED IN 'A LITTLE REALM OF THE RIGHTEOUS'

Jonah's limitations are the product of his own heritage. His world view has been formed by Mosaic Law – the law he has been brought up to revere and adhere to. But being shaped by our past does not excuse us from changing direction in the future. Christ, whom Jonah prefigures in so many ways, will preach radical change, radical equality and radical love. He will warn against putting new wine into old wineskins. New wine is a living thing: it ferments in the wineskins, which have to be new and supple to accommodate it. If we are closed to new ideas, if we adhere blindly to the world view we have always held, we are old wineskins which can only accommodate old wine.

Jesus railed at the fact that God's law was buried under the hair-splitting legalism of the Scribes and Pharisees. The rigidity of their approach stifled the spirit of the law. Jesus saw it as a presumptuous attempt by men to put limits around God's wisdom and mercy. He reminded his followers that the principle is greater than the law intended to promote it – 'the sabbath is made for humankind, not humankind for the sabbath' (Mk 2:27). At the same time, Jesus made it clear that he did not come to overthrow the law, but to complete it. Far from undermining the law, Jesus makes greater demands on it than did Moses: referring to the Ten Commandments, he said, 'You have heard that it was said to those of ancient times, "You shall not murder"... But I say to you that if you are angry with a brother or sister, you will be liable to judgement' (Mt 5:21, 22). Jesus' view of the law is distilled from what he saw as the greatest of the Commandments – to love God, and to love our neighbour as ourselves; 'On these two commandments hang all the law and the prophets' (Mt 22:40).

Sometimes it is easier to keep legal specifics than to love. Sometimes it is easier to live within clearly defined limits than to let the Spirit fill the sails of our soul and take us where he will. Jonah did not have the benefit of Christ's teaching to guide him, but he had the word of God speaking unequivocally in his ear. The reverse is true for us. The end result is the same: we, like Jonah, must lift ourselves out of our comfort zone and obey the two greatest commandments.

God asks the fuming Jonah, 'Do you do well to be angry for the plant?' to which Jonah, true to form, replies, 'I do well to be angry, angry enough to die'. God says, in the closing verses of the Book of Jonah:

You pity the plant, for which you did not labour, and which you did not grow; it came into being in a night and perished in a night. And should not I not be concerned about Nineveh, that great city, in which there are more than 120,000 persons who do not know their right hand from their left, and also many cattle?

Jonah remains silent. He has failed to understand that his role as a prophet of God is not to repudiate or to vanquish evil, but to transform it. A modern Jewish philosopher, Martin Buber, asks:

Are we to establish a little realm of the righteous and leave the rest to the Lord? Is it for this that he gave us a mouth to convey the truth of our heart to an alien heart and a hand which can communicate to the hand of our recalcitrant brother something of the warmth of our very blood?[6]

The God who saved Jonah and spared the Ninevites is the God who is everywhere, even in the depths of Sheol. To quote Buber again:

Evil and good, despair and hope, the power of destruction and the power of rebirth, dwell side by side. The divine force which man actually encounters in life does not hover above the demonic, but penetrates it.[7]

Nineveh repents and is saved on this occasion. The change of heart is short-lived; the Ninevites will revert to their corrupt and cruel ways and the city will ultimately be destroyed. Only the animals will inhabit it, in a desolation vividly evoked by the prophet Zephaniah:

> Herds shall lie down in it,
> even wild animals;
> the desert-owl and the screech-owl
> shall lodge on its capitals;
> the owl shall hoot at the window,
> the raven croak on the threshold. (Zeph 2:14)

But there was one moment in the city's bloody history when it repented, and that moment is preserved forever by Jonah and by Christ: 'The people of Nineveh will rise up at the judgement with this generation and condemn it, because they repented at the proclamation of Jonah, and see, something greater than Jonah is here!' (Lk 11:32) That moment is made eternally present by Christ and reminds us that nothing is entirely evil. If called, we must still go to Nineveh.

'And should not I not be concerned about Nineveh, that great city, in which there are more than 120,000 persons who do not know their right hand from their left, and also many cattle?' (Was God touched, too, by the endearing notion of the repentant animals?) This is the last sentence of the book. It ends mid-conversation, waiting for Jonah's answer.

The law given to Moses by God was intended as a means to an end – a framework to help people to live good and upright lives. For the Jews at the time of Jonah (and for generations thereafter) a rigid adherence to the Torah, the Law, was a vital element in preserving ethnic, ethical, religious and cultural identity – consistently under threat from foreign occupation. The Torah was the mortar that cemented the relationship between the Chosen People and their God. However, the law that should liberate can often confine. I am not so very different to Jonah. I, too, often find it very easy to stay caged in Buber's 'little realm of the righteous'. The law which was given to Moses as a springboard for experiencing God's love can too easily become a treadmill. Instead of letting ourselves be stretched by its spirit, we can allow ourselves to atrophy in observance of the letter of the law. Devotion becomes legalism and we fall into the trap of making unforgiving distinctions between those who are and are not 'acceptable'.

I can usefully ask myself questions that Jonah should have been asking. What am I running from today? What is God asking of me that I don't do? In what way do I need to change my attitudes in order to become a channel of God's love? What is my Nineveh? Who am I judging, and whose repentance am I evaluating? Am I really so free from the audacity of deciding who deserves forgiveness and who does not?

I, too, have experienced the storms and the drought that God sends to attract my attention. God approaches me with the same love and logic – even the same playfulness – with which he approached Jonah. He will not let me go, as he did not let Jonah go, and as he did not let Nineveh go. His question to me, like his question to Jonah, is waiting for my answer. So I pray, in the words of Matheson's great hymn:

> O Love that wilt not let me go,
> I rest my weary soul in thee;
> I give thee back the life I owe,

That in thine ocean depths its flow
May richer, fuller be.

NOTES

1   Carlo Collodi, *The Adventures of Pinocchio*, New York, Macmillan, 1926, p. 363.

2   Hosea, Joel, Amos, Obadiah, Jonah, Micah, Nahum, Habakkuk, Haggai, Zechariah and Malachi. The term 'minor' refers to the shorter length of these books and not their importance.

3   David Daniel Luckenbill, *Ancient Records of Assyria and Babylonia*, Chicago, University of Chicago Press, 1926, pp. 146–7.

4   Rabbi Alexandra Wright, Yom Kippur Sermon 2006 at Liberal Jewish Synagogue, London, accessed at Liberal Jewish Synagogue website: www.ljs.org.

5   Martin Luther, *Lectures on the Minor Prophets: Jonah and Habakkuk*, St Louis, Concordia Publishing House, 1974, pp. 91–2.

6   Martin Buber, *Eclipse of God, Studies in the Relation between Religion and Philosophy*, New York, Harper & Brothers, 1952, p. 31.

7   Quoted by Maurice S. Friedman, *Martin Buber: The Life of Dialogue*, London, Routledge, 2002, p. 162.

4

THE FORCE FIELD OF THE PAST

'REMEMBER LOT'S WIFE'

Besides this, you know what time it is, how it is now the moment for you to wake from sleep. For salvation is nearer to us now than when we first became believers; the night is far gone, the day is near.

Romans 13:11, 12

THE FORCE FIELD OF THE PAST

'Remember Lot's wife' (Lk 17:32). In three stark words Jesus takes us back to the book of Genesis and to a woman whose name we do not know, and whose words have never been recorded. Yet who does not remember her bizarre fate? It is described in fourteen words: 'But Lot's wife, behind him, looked back, and she became a pillar of salt.' (Gen 19:26)

I was very young when I first encountered the story of Lot's wife, accompanied by an old woodcut which vividly depicted her fate. Across the passage of many years, I can see that black and white picture with astonishing clarity. In the foreground Lot and his daughters are hurrying upward, away from the sulphurous blast which is laying waste to the landscape behind them. The entire background is occupied by blinding sheets of light, suggesting the cataclysm taking place below. Most chilling of all to my child's eye, however, was the still grey figure of Lot's wife in the centre of the picture. Even as her upper body is in the act of turning, her feet are already frozen forever. It was a shocking evocation of instantaneous, brutal retribution.

As I became more familiar with the story in later years, my puzzlement intensified. Lot's wife's offence seems to pale in comparison with the activities of her deeply unpleasant husband. Yet he is spared, to commit further disgraceful acts. What was so terrible about his wife disobeying a command not to look back?

When I first saw the picture, I couldn't understand why Lot's wife would have wanted to turn back in the first place. But then, at that time in my life, I was untouched by the force field of the past. Forty years or so later, my perspective has changed. I now understand – through my own experience and that of others – what it can be to be imprisoned by the past. The shackles can take many forms – nostalgia, remorse, resentment, an overwhelming attachment to things and places. The past is so safe – a finite thing, defined in space and time, containing no surprises. How often do we seek security rather than fulfilment? How often are we frozen between where we have been (and perhaps should never have been) and where we should go?

The past is like an old shoe – it may not be ideal for a long journey, but it requires no breaking in and slips on easily. Even the unhappiness of the past can be more comfortable than engaging with the present, while happy memories can hold us indefinitely in their thrall. An old grievance, an old triumph, an old love, an old resentment – we go back, we replay events, relive them, rewrite them.

An attachment to the past, a reluctance to live in the present – these may not be conductive to spiritual growth, but are they really such heinous offences? In an effort to understand, I decided to walk in Lot's unattractive company and see whether there was anything familiar in the moral landscape through which the journey brought me.

THE JOURNEY TO BETHEL

The small Palestinian hillside village of Beitin is situated in the West Bank, about ten miles north of Jerusalem. It has a population of about 2,000 and today its only claim to fame lies in the fruitfulness of its olive, almond, fig and plum trees. It is hard to believe that a city once stood here, the thriving Canaanite city of Bethel – mentioned sixty-six times in the Old Testament. Bethel was at that time named Luz ('almond tree'). Jacob, who had his 'ladder' vision here, renamed it Beth-El – 'house of God'.

About a mile east of Beitin, a vista opens up over the Jordan Valley. Jericho, the oldest continuously inhabited city in the world, lies below, some eleven miles or so away. Far beneath is the Dead Sea, the lowest point of the earth – over 1,200 feet below the level of the Mediterranean, only some miles away to the west. Across the shimmering salt waters the hills of Moab rise to the east, reaching a height of 4,400 feet over the Dead Sea at Mount Nebo (or Pisgah) – from whose summit the dying Moses gazed across at the Promised Land. Over five hundred years before the birth of Moses, Jacob's grandfather Abraham, then called 'Abram', pitched his tent here for a while after God had called him to leave his own country. Born in Ur in what was then northern Mesopotamia, Abraham moved with his large household – including his nephew Lot – on a series of family migrations which took them from Ur to Haran, then on to Bethel and the Negev in southern Palestine. Finally, driven by famine, they arrived in Egypt, where Abraham prospered. By the time Abraham returned to Bethel, he was 'very rich in livestock, in silver and in gold ... and Lot, who went with Abram, also had flocks and herds and tents' (Gen 13:2, 5).

At this point, the ways of Abraham and Lot parted. Their flocks were so numerous that it had become difficult to provide grazing for them. Their herdsmen had begun to quarrel and Abraham suggested that it would be better if they lived apart. Standing somewhere along this little stretch of road between Beitin and Et-Tell Abraham – although the senior of the two – offered Lot his choice of the surrounding country. Lot 'looked about him and saw that the plain of the Jordan was well watered everywhere like the garden of the Lord ... so Lot chose for himself all of the plain of the Jordan' (Gen 13:10, 11). 'How awesome is this place! This is none other than the house of God, and this is the gate of heaven!' Jacob said of Bethel after his vision there. For Lot it would be the gateway to somewhere very different.

CHASMS – PHYSICAL AND MORTAL

It is difficult to imagine a starker contrast between what Lot saw and what can be seen today. Instead of a lush green plain, one of the most desolate and inhospitable areas on the face of the earth stretches out below.

This region has one of the largest geological fault systems in the world, separating the African and the Arabian tectonic plates. It is a continuation of the Great Rift Valley which runs all the way from Mozambique, 4,000 kilometres away. Flanked by towering escarpments on the east and west, the rift valley created by the Dead Sea fault is one of the deepest and most abrupt depressions on Earth. Here is the point at which a continent broke, twenty or thirty million years ago, when huge tectonic forces pulled the earth apart and separated Africa from Arabia. The Dead Sea Valley became the main land route out of Africa for the first hominids (in this context it is interesting that one of the favoured locations for the biblical Garden of Eden is the Jordan Valley). The massive tectonic plates are still pulling apart. In this highly unstable environment, the five Cities of the Plain were built. Their foundations were laid on silt and sand – the sand which would liquefy so disastrously in the events to come.

As Lot took his first steps towards Sodom, none of this was apparent. The Cities of the Plain, especially Sodom, were substantial and fortified. The land around was richly productive. There was significant movement of people throughout the region and a busy trade was conducted from city to city – not just within the Jordan Valley but throughout the Fertile Crescent – the great arc of arable land which stretched from the Persian Gulf to the eastern shores of the Mediterranean. Studies of fossilised plants in this area show that a wide variety of crops was grown, including barley, wheat, grapes, figs, lentils, flax, chickpeas, peas, broad beans, dates and olives. Nothing in this flourishing and abundant scene hinted at the yawning cavity on which it rested.

Lot was equally oblivious of the moral chasm within himself. When he looked across the Jordan Valley to the uplands on the east side of the Dead Sea, he had no inkling that these would one day be named for his son Moab, whom he would father incestuously with his eldest daughter, and that the land of Ammon between Moab and the Arabian desert would be named for the son he would conceive with his younger daughter.

Lot now made the first move in the journey which would end so ignominiously in a cave above Zoar, one of the five infamous Cities of the Plain. He went down to the fertile plain and 'moved his tent as far as Sodom', which was already notorious for its wickedness (Gen 13:12,13). This 'wickedness' is variously described in the Bible: 'Sodom ... had pride, excess of food, and prosperous ease, but did not aid the poor and needy. They were haughty and did abominable things before me' (Ezek 16:49, 50) and 'Sodom and Gomorrah and the surrounding cities ... indulged in sexual immorality and pursued unnatural lust' (Jude 7). Abraham took the harder road, making his way to the heights of Hebron, where he settled by the great oaks of Mamre (this area is one of the worst flashpoints in today's volatile West Bank, where Jews and Muslims live cheek by jowl and where the refusal to let go of the past creates ongoing turmoil).

It is always easier to move down than up. Lot must have known the reputation of the Cities of the Plain, but he probably told himself that he could resist temptation. After all, he wasn't planning to live in Sodom – only to camp nearby, where he could avail of the commercial opportunities such a thriving city offered. He wasn't planning to expose his family to the degenerate lifestyle of the inhabitants, or to have his children assimilate their heathen ways. The next we hear of Lot, he has moved into the city of Sodom itself (Gen 14:12). It is so easy to move almost imperceptibly across the boundaries we have set ourselves. To shift our moral landscape.

Canaan, when Abraham and Lot lived there, was not a unified country but was a collection of city-states into which the Amorites had been pouring. This fierce nomadic tribe gradually set themselves up as kings of a number of cities which formerly belonged to the Ur dynasty. By 1830 BC they had founded the first dynasty of Babylon. Local kings paid tribute to them but at the time of Abraham and Lot the kings of the Cities of the Plain rebelled against their overlords. In the ensuing war, the kings of Sodom and Gomorrah were routed and fled to the mountains. The Amorites sacked the cities and took Lot captive, with his wife, his people and his goods.

Word of Lot's plight reached Abraham at Mamre. He immediately took 318 trained men of his household and went into battle to free Lot and all his household. As he made his way home from the battlefield, the king of Sodom came to meet Abraham on the way. The king begged Abraham to return Lot and his people to him: 'Give me the persons, but take the goods for yourself.' (Gen 14:21) Clearly, Lot had become a man of substance in the eyes of Sodom. Abraham scornfully replied that he wouldn't accept as much as a shoelace from the king of Sodom, while Lot promptly removed himself from Abraham's influence, and returned to Sodom. Was the king's flattering concern for him too sharp a contrast with his uncle's real or imagined censure?

Resisting rescue

Sometimes our attachment to the past is so powerful that we blind ourselves to God's hand in our lives. There are times when a seeming disaster conceals the hand of God's providence, if we have only the faith – or the will – to see it. We, like Lot, have sometimes been pulled out of Sodom, and some of us – also like Lot – have returned there once the storm has passed. Others, more clear-sighted, have recognised a turning point and have gone forward instead of back.

The next mention of Lot comes when Abraham is warned by the Lord of the imminent destruction of the Cities of the Plain. Abraham pleads with the Lord not to destroy Sodom. Two angels are sent to Sodom and are received by Lot, whom they encounter 'sitting in the gate of Sodom'. This is the place where elders of the city conduct their business and attend to legal matters. Lot's presence there reinforces the suggestion that he is now a well assimilated member of the community. The days when this nomadic herdsman camped near the town are clearly long gone – he has a house within the city walls, where he entertains his guests. His daughters are betrothed to men of the city.

We don't suddenly wake up one morning to find that we have strayed a long way from God. It happens by degrees. Little by little we lower our standards and compromise our faith, without ever realising that the vitality and strength has gone out of our belief, and has decayed into an empty formalism. Lot, in his position of authority at the city gate, can seldom have felt more secure. He has no inkling that this is to be his last night in Sodom. He rises to meet the visitors, and offers his home as lodging before they go on their way. After they arrive at his home, he prepares a feast for them. But this is rudely interrupted when the men of the city gather at Lot's door, demanding that his visitors be brought out to them 'that we may know them' (Gen 19:5). In an action which must have taken bravery, Lot goes out to the mob, shutting the door behind him and says, 'I beg you, brothers, do not act so wickedly'. However, after the first rush of courage, he hastily adds, 'Behold, I have two daughters who have not known a man; let me bring them out to you, and do to them as you please; only do nothing to these men, for they have come under the shelter of my roof'.

This is the man who is spared by God while his wife is turned into a pillar of salt! It is hard to reconcile this behaviour with Peter's description of Lot as a righteous man, tormented in his soul by the men of Sodom's lawless deeds (2 Pet 2:8). The only hint the Genesis narrative gives us that he is in any way uncomfortable with life in Sodom comes when the men of Sodom refuse the offer of the daughters and cry out, 'This fellow came here as an alien, and he would play the judge! Now we will deal worse with you than with them'. The angels rescue Lot and stress the need to get out of Sodom before it is destroyed. Lot is in no hurry to leave. With destruction at his very door, he lingers yet another night.

It is so easy for us to linger, and we can do so until our death, letting the noise of the world drown out the voice of God. Sometimes, mercifully, God rescues us against our will – sometimes even more than once, as he did with Lot. Lot had once been taken by force from Sodom, when he was captured by the Mesopotamians. Now he, his wife and his daughters have to be dragged bodily out of the city by the angels: 'But he lingered; so the men seized him and his wife and his two daughters by the hand, the Lord being merciful to him, and they brought him out and set him outside the city.' (Gen 19:16) The angels tell Lot, 'Flee for your life; do not look back or stop anywhere in the Plain; flee to the hills, or else you will be consumed'. Even now, Lot baulks. He doesn't believe that he can make it to safety in the hills and he asks to stay on the plain:

> Oh, no, my lords; behold, your servant has found favour with you, and you have shown me great kindness in saving my life; but I cannot flee to the hills, for fear the disaster will overtake me, and I die. Look, that city is near enough to flee to, and it is a little one. Let me escape there – is it not a little one? – and my life will be saved! (Gen 19:18-20)

I have done that too – bargained with God. 'Yes, thank you for saving me from this particular evil, but don't ask me to renounce everything!' Some of the great saints have not been immune from this – we have only to remember St Augustine: 'Make me chaste and continent, but not yet.'[1]

With continuing forbearance, the angels agree to spare the particular city identified by Lot, which is called Zoar. Then, as Lot and his family are leaving, the cataclysm erupts. There is no evidence of a volcanic eruption in this area at the time of Sodom and Gomorrah, but plenty of indications of earthquake activity. Twentieth-century geological studies[2] suggest that subterranean combustible materials destroyed the cities. Bitumen and petroleum have been found in the area, along with natural gas and sulphur. It is believed that a whole section of the earth's crust slipped along the fault, resulting in a massive earthquake. The terrific pressure of the shifting mass would have forced the oils and gases upward through the earth. If these highly flammable deposits were ignited by a spark – or by lightening – as they were forced through the fault line, the resulting explosion would almost certainly have the effect of raining fire and brimstone. Meanwhile, the force of the quake caused the earth to liquefy and collapse inwards, literally swallowing the cities.

While Lot and his daughters are still struggling towards Zoar, Abraham goes to the place where he had stood before the Lord 'and he looked down towards Sodom and Gomorrah and toward all the land of the plain, and saw the smoke of the land going up like the smoke of a furnace' (Gen 19:28).

Archaeological findings at Bab edh-Dhra and Numeira at the south-east of the Dead Sea are now commonly thought to be the remains of Sodom and Gomorrah.[3] Both places were destroyed by an enormous conflagration, leaving ash and debris several feet thick. The site at Bab edh-Dhra was a fortified city, its walls enclosing an area of about ten acres. The north-east gate – possibly the one in which Lot sat – had two flanking towers with massive stone and timber foundations. The estimated population was in the region of 1,200. A remarkable feature is the huge burial ground containing 20,000 tombs – this was clearly the cemetery for a number of cities, and perhaps also for the large nomadic population which traversed this once fertile land.

Bab edh-Dhra, Numeira and all the surrounding countryside remained uninhabited for a thousand years after they were destroyed. As Lot and his family fled the cataclysmic upheaval in

Sodom, Lot's wife looked back and became a pillar of salt. Why the terrible fate?

FROZEN BY THE PAST

She looked back. This is reinforced by the context in which Christ refers to her. As described by Luke, the Pharisees have raised the question about the coming of the Kingdom of God and Jesus answers them briefly. Then he turns to his own followers and elaborates:

> ... on the day that Lot left Sodom, it rained fire and sulphur from heaven and destroyed them all – it will be like that on the day when the Son of Man is revealed. On that day, anyone on the housetop who has belongings in the house must not come down to take them away; and likewise anyone in the field must not turn back. Remember Lot's wife. Those who try to make their life secure will lose it, but those who lose their life will keep it. (Lk 17:29-33)

The downfall of Lot's wife was her refusal to believe that she *could* walk away. When Christ speaks of the desire to save one's life, he is speaking of a desire to preserve *our own definition* of life. Very often, we see life in terms of who we are, what we do and what we possess. Our energies go into preserving the illusion of control over all of this. To 'lose' this life is to relinquish control, to allow ourselves, in the words of the twelfth-century Hildegard of Bingen, to be 'blown like a feather on the breath of God'. Lot's wife was unable to trust herself to trust God. In seeking to hold on to her life as she knew it, she lost everything.

It is to *his own followers*, not to the Pharisees, that Jesus emphasises the lack of preparedness in which many will be found. They follow him, listen to him, love him, and still he feels he has to warn them (I am reminded again of St Augustine, or, at least, of a saying attributed to him and famously quoted by Beckett in *Waiting for Godot*: 'Do not despair; one of the thieves was saved. Do not presume; one of the thieves was damned').

The 'day when the Son of Man is revealed' is not necessarily the last day – either of the world or of our own life. It can be a time when God's will is made clear to us. For Lot's wife, the day she left Sodom was for her 'the day when the Son of Man is revealed'. She now knew unequivocally that the life she had lived in Sodom was destructive. She heard the words of warning, but clearly did not believe them. Lot was afraid of the future, but his wife was afraid of leaving the past behind her and that was the greater danger.

Lot's wife couldn't move forward because of the pull of the past. She couldn't even move back. And many of us have been Lot's wife too – frozen into immobility. I have been on the housetop when the Lord gave a warning I could not fail to hear, and yet I turned back into the house despite the warning to leave everything. What is it that pulls me back into the house? What is it that lets me hear the call of God and still linger? How many times have I put my hand to the plough and still turned back? The door through which the Lord calls me is always open, but on my last day on earth it will close forever. Which side of the door will I be on then?

Lot's wife looked back. It wasn't a passing glance. The verb 'to look' in the original ancient Hebrew verb is the same as that used by God when he tells Abraham to look into the sky and count the stars, and promises him that his descendants will be as numerous as these. Clearly, no casual glance is intended here. Some translations read she looked back longingly[4] or 'expectingly'[5] (Gen 19:17). Lot has left Sodom empty-handed. All the riches and status he has accumulated are consumed in the furnace. He has left fearfully, reluctantly, but at least he has managed to leave. His wife initially obeyed the call to 'flee for your life'. She didn't join her sons-in-law in mocking Lot's message. She set off with Lot, but her heart was in Sodom. 'Where your treasure is, there your heart will be also.' (Mt 6:21) She looks back, not in idle curiosity, but in yearning for all that is being left behind. She couldn't let go, even to save her life.

What lay ahead held no attraction. She had left the hardships of the nomadic life behind her many years earlier. The city, with its luxuries and perhaps its lusts, was where her heart lay. Like the heavy drinker or smoker for whom the prospect of sickness and death is preferable to letting the substance go, life would be unthinkable without it. She stops and turns, and is annihilated along with the city. Like the city, she is destroyed from within.

SUPPRESSING THE MOVEMENT OF TURNING

The influence of the past is at its most dangerous when we see ourselves as shaped by past forces beyond the reach of our will and our understanding. 'The experience of my past has made me what I am today', we tell ourselves. 'My world view has been determined for me. No matter how much I would like to, I cannot look at life differently.' Maybe Lot's wife said something like this to herself, 'This is all I know of life. I can't leave it'. Thus we excuse our inaction, our distractions, our refusal to let go of attachment or resentment or guilt or fear. Our gaze is bent relentlessly backward. Yet we need to bear in mind that, while we may not be able to change how we *feel*, we *can* change the way we act.

Lot, for all his faults, was not afraid to keep listening to the Lord. He may not have wanted to leave Sodom but what he *felt* didn't matter: the fact is that he *did* leave. He went empty-handed out of Sodom into the unknown. His wife could not bring herself to trust in God and her refusal to move destroyed her as she became 'a pillar of salt standing as a monument to an unbelieving soul' (Wis 10:7). Not a *disobedient* soul – but an *unbelieving* soul. As Martin Buber writes:

> The only thing that can become fate for a man is belief in fate; for this suppresses the movement of turning ... to be freed from belief that there is no freedom is indeed to be free.[6]

For each of us, there is a 'day when the Son of Man is revealed' in a call to repentance, to growth, to transformation. If we are to heed that call and advance on our journey, we have to take ourselves out of the comfort zone of what *was* and enter the adventure of what *is*. We cannot make a journey if we are facing backwards. Lot may have felt terrified, but he did go forward – even though the journey ended in ignominy.

Lot 'was afraid to stay in Zoar' (Gen 19:30), and eventually does what he was first instructed to do. He goes up into the hills. There he lives in a cave above the city with his two daughters. His

inglorious history ends with the episode where his daughters –
fearing that the world has been destroyed and that this is their
only chance to procreate – get him drunk and sleep with him.
They each bear a son: one becomes the ancestor of the Moabites
and the other of the Ammonites – both tribes become enemies of
Israel and are excluded from the congregation of Israel (Deut 23:3).

Out of small movements in the right direction, great things
can come. It is true that the enemy tribes of Moab and Ammon,
thorns in Israel's side for many centuries, had their origin in that
sordid episode in the hilltop cave above Zoar. But a radiant
alliance between Israelites and Moabites will be forged
generations later at Bethlehem, twenty miles north of where
Abraham stood at Mamre witnessing the fall of Sodom. Ruth
the Moabitess will come to Bethlehem with her mother-in-law,
Naomi. She will glean barley in the field of Boaz, will marry him
and become the great grandmother of King David, and the
ancestress of Jesus of Nazareth.

> Friend, hope for the Guest while you are alive.
> Jump into experience while you are alive!
> Think ... and think ... while you are alive.
> What you call 'salvation' belongs to the time before death.
>
> If you don't break your ropes while you're alive,
> do you think ghosts will do it after?[7]

NOTES

1 St Augustine, *Confessions*, Book 8, Chapter 7, Signet Classics, 2001, p. 164.

2 F.G. Clapp, 'The Site of Sodom and Gomorrah', *American Journal of Archaeology*, Vol. 40, No. 3 (1936), pp. 323–44; G.M. Harris and A.P. Beardow, 'The destruction of Sodom and Gomorrah: a geotechnical perspective', *Quarterly Journal of Engineering Geology*, Vol. 28, No. 4 (1995); David Neev, K.O. Emery, *The Destruction of Sodom, Gomorrah, and Jericho: Geological, Climatological, and Archaeological Background*, New York, Oxford University Press, 1995.

3 Between 1973 and 1979 two archaeologists, Walter E. Rast and R. Thomas Schaub, surveyed an area around the south-east of the Dead Sea and located the remains of five sites, each at the head of a small and dry riverbed.

4 *New English Translation* (NET).

5 *Young's Literal Translation* (YLT).

6 Martin Buber, *I and Thou*, New York, Continuum, 2004, p. 48.

7 'The Time Before Death' by Kabir (fifteenth-century Indian mystic) in an anthology compiled by Robert Bly, *The Soul is Here for its Own Joy*, New York, Ecco, 1999, p. 81.

5

LETTING OUR CHILDREN GO

HANNAH

> The place is too narrow for me; make room for me to
> dwell in!
>
> Isaiah 49:20[1]

THE HOUSE OF TOMORROW

In 1 Kings 3 we read the famous story of Solomon's judgement in relation to the two women claiming to be the mother of the one child. When Solomon ordered the baby to be divided between the women, the true mother cried out, 'Please, my lord, give her the living boy; certainly do not kill him!' It is an extreme example of the necessity of letting a child go in order to keep it.

Like a number of biblical women – Sarah the mother of Isaac, Hannah the mother of Samuel, Elizabeth the mother of John the Baptist, and the unnamed mother of Samson – I came relatively late to motherhood. By an extraordinary coincidence, three of these women featured in the liturgy readings for the week of my daughter's birth: Samson's mother on 19 December, Hannah on 22 December and Elizabeth on 23 December, our daughter's actual birthday. At Mass in the chill pre-dawn on 22

December my heart sang with Hannah, whose song was the Psalm for that day, 'My heart exults in the Lord'.

Like Jesus after them, Samson, Samuel and John made their way from darkness into light, from the confinement of the womb into the amplitude of the world. They were wrapped in swaddling clothes as babies have been from time immemorial, and as newborn babies are to this day. The technique that I learned was a simpler one than that which the women of the Bible used, but the principle was the same: to provide warmth and security for a baby who has just left the closeness of the womb.

When our baby's umbilical cord was cut, my husband said how conscious he was of the significance of that moment, which established her new, separate existence. For me, the feeling was the reverse; I was suddenly, and forever, bound to her. I was not 'delivered of' a child, but 'delivered to' her. As her separate existence began, mine ended. There would never be a time thereafter when what she did or suffered or thrilled to would not affect me too. 'Can a mother forget her nursing child?' asks Isaiah (49:15).

I had to – and have to – remind myself that while my heart belongs to her, she does not belong to me. In the words of Kahlil Gibran's *The Prophet*, our children

> ... come through you but not from you. And though they are with you yet they belong not to you. You may give them your love but not your thoughts, for they have their own thoughts. You may house their bodies but not their souls, for their souls dwell in the house of tomorrow.[2]

It isn't long before a baby no longer needs the security of swaddling clothes. A healthy baby is in continual motion. Before he is even able to roll and turn he is stretching, kicking, wriggling; the tiny fists punch into the air, the little feet pedal furiously. He is like a swimmer in an invisible medium, pushing now against and now with the current. Once a swimmer stops moving, he sinks; once a bird stops flying, it falls. Our babies learn early that motion is their natural state, as it is the natural state of our spinning planet, of our universe, and of the 'divine milieu' in which and for which our souls exist.

For parents, there is a dual challenge: knowing when the time has come to let our children go, and not being afraid to hold on to them until that time has come. The latter challenge is increasing as the culture of instant gratification takes hold in the western world. Gibran's 'house of tomorrow' is easily displaced by a greedy 'today'. The abrasive and thought-provoking psychoanalyst and writer, David Smail, speaks of an increasingly prevalent situation in which children are left to grow up like weeds as their parents resist any distraction from their own quest for personal satisfaction. He describes the situation as one of indifference to the fate of the next generation:

> It seems more and more to be the case that parents are coming to experience their children as a threat to their emotional peace and independence, as yet more competition for scarce satisfactions, so that adult power comes to serve the struggle for personal 'happiness' more than cultivation of a future for our progeny.[3]

However, for most well-meaning parents, the real task is to recognise when the time has arrived to let our children go beyond the confines of our own lives. Isaiah's words ring down through the millennia in the age-old cry: 'The place is too narrow for me; make room for me to dwell in!' (Is 49:20)[4] The extent to which we have ourselves advanced, have 'grown up', is largely the extent to which we will be capable of letting our own children go. The longing for the warmth and security of the womb can hold us in an infantile state; a culture of instant gratification can help keep us there.

Sooner or later, many of us stop moving forward. We reach a point of our development which seems relatively safe. We settle for a modest degree of success and of comfort. We stop at the oasis, rather than push on across the wilderness to the Promised Land. We swaddle ourselves in familiarity, and we risk binding our children too. Smail puts it very succinctly:

> We settle for that point of our development beyond which we dare not advance, and we elaborate a life out of the safe knowledge thus far gained ... We tend to traumatise our children early; rather than trying all we can to use our adult knowledge and power to stand in their position and make sense for them of *their* experience, to make space in which they can act from their own perspective, we tend to impose upon them a cold objective gaze which monitors their every departure from *our* norms and enables us to force them back into the ways of our choosing.[5]

Our own fear of the unknown is what can make us hold our children back. If we are not confident in the future and in our own ability to move forward, it is very likely that we will transfer that anxiety to our children. The desire to protect them can be a crippling force. But it is not an irresistible one.

Hannah's song of joy resonated with me on the morning before our daughter's birth. However, in later years when I revisited the book of Samuel, I found that Hannah was full of surprises. Hers was a complex and fascinating story and one which came to be filled with significance for me as my own child grew.

FROM OBSCURITY TO EMPIRE

Hannah's song of praise – so strongly echoed in the Magnificat – which I took to be the natural joy of a mother expecting a longed-for baby is actually sung three years after her son's birth, when she hands him over to Eli the priest, to serve the Lord in the temple. 'For this child I prayed, and the Lord granted me the petition that I made to him. Therefore I have lent him to the Lord; as long as he lives, he is given to the Lord.' (1 Sam 1:27) She prepares to return to a home in which her child will never again shout and laugh and play. Her contact with Samuel thereafter is described in a few pathetic words: 'And his mother used to make for him a little robe and take it to him each year, when she went up with her husband to offer the yearly sacrifice' (1 Sam 2:19). That she can sing this exultant hymn through her heartbreak indicates an extraordinary faith and a strong sense of her son's destiny.

Who was she, this obscure woman from the hill country? She was the childless first wife of Elkanah, of the tribe of Ephraim.

Elkanah had two wives; the second, Peninnah, had several children and taunted Hannah year in, year out with her childlessness. Peninnah's vitriol probably stemmed from the fact that, though infertile, Hannah was dearly loved by her husband. Hannah's interaction with Elkanah and his shrewish second wife suggests that she was gentle, loving and sweet-tempered. Like another humble – but by no means falsely humble – young woman centuries later, she described herself as God's 'handmaid'. On one of their annual visits to the temple at Shiloh, Hannah, deeply distressed, poured out her heart to the Lord and begged him to give her a son:

> O Lord of hosts, if only you will look on the misery of your servant and remember me, and not forget your servant, but will give to your servant a male child, then I will set him before you as one consecrated until the day of his death. (1 Sam 1:11).

This sentence is remarkable, as it is the first time in Scripture that God is addressed by the title 'god of hosts'.[6] This becomes a popular name for God in the later prophetic books of the Bible, where the title evokes God as the supreme king of all powers, earthly and heavenly, who has triumphed over all his enemies. The word 'hosts' comes from the Hebrew 'Zeba'ot' or 'Sabaoth' and has a military connotation. It is a strange phrase for Hannah to use – especially as, at the time she lived, Israel was in chaos. After entering the Promised Land, a long period of violence and decline had ensued. Ruled by six successive judges, Israel was ravaged by war with the Edomites, the Moabites and – at the time Hannah lived – the Philistines. When Samuel was born, the great and flawed Samson was probably the ruling judge. The book of Judges has a recurring motif: 'In those days there was no king in Israel; all the people did what was right in their own eyes.'

Political chaos was matched by spiritual decay: the sons of Eli the priest at the temple in Shiloh that Hannah visits are worthless and degenerate, abusing their priestly privileges in the basest way. Their father makes only half-hearted efforts to restrain them. The prevailing spiritual climate is summed up in the sombre sentence: 'And the word of the Lord was rare in those days; visions were not widespread.' (1 Sam 3:1)

Hannah bursts upon this scene of apathy and decline with her arresting phrase 'Lord of hosts' and her triumphant and prophetic canticle: 'My heart exults in the Lord; my horn is exalted in the Lord.' (The word used in modern translations is 'strength'; the literal translation is 'horn'. Zechariah will use the image in Luke 1:69 when he prophesies at the birth of John the Baptist.) Because the strength of an ox or a ram could be expressed in its horn, the horn is often used as a picture of strength in the Bible (Ps 18:2, 75:4-5, 92:10; Jer 48:25). Hannah is speaking of her power being exalted in the Lord.

God's faithfulness in the past is her assurance of his faithfulness in the future, and in this powerful conviction she hands her first-born son to God. Her canticle of praise is the longest speech by a woman in Scripture. It is a remarkable and immensely prophetic song. In using the word 'rock' to describe God (2:2) Hannah becomes the first person since Moses to do so; he used it no less than seven times in his final song on Mount Pisgah, within sight of the Promised Land. Hannah, like Moses, is standing on the threshold of enormous transition in Israel. She sings of a world turned upside down, where the weak triumph, the poor are made rich, and the lowly are exalted. It is revolutionary theology, which will be echoed by Mary in the Magnificat and fulfilled by Christ. (Familiarity may have blunted us to the incendiary nature of these canticles, but as recently as the 1980s the government of Guatemala banned the public recitation of the Magnificat because of its subversive message.)[7]

The closing lines of Hannah's song are the most remarkable of all: 'The Lord will judge the ends of the earth; he will give strength to his king, and exalt the power of his anointed.' (1 Sam 2:10) Hannah cannot know that her son will anoint Israel's first king and will institute the Davidic monarchy, as Elizabeth's son – centuries later – will be the forerunner for the King of Kings. She does not know that this toddler will, over the years to come, help forge a fragmented and enfeebled people into a great empire. Instead of being governed by judges at Shiloh, Israel will be ruled by kings at Jerusalem. As she hands her son over to the Lord, one story is ending and another is beginning. Hannah's canticle indicates that she recognises she is standing at a turning point in history; she, like Mary after her, willingly becomes a channel for God's transformative work. Every parent is potentially such a channel.

There is always something selfish in our love for our children – no matter how wonderful they are, we love them chiefly because they are ours. Their kindness, their beauty, their talent are an enhanced reflection of ourselves. Their failures and shortcomings are our own disappointments. The things that make us angriest in them are our own faults; the things that make us proudest are sometimes the things in which we have been less than successful. The relationship is almost redemptive – in helping them become better than we have been, we redeem our own past failings. The relationship is powerful, emotional, intellectual, visceral. Our children take root so deeply in our heart that it seems the heart will be torn out of us when they go.

CROSSING THE RIVER OF LOSS

The ability of a baby to separate from his mother is an essential part of growing up. It is a difficult enough process – but made many times more difficult if the mother refuses to separate from her child. The American poet Mary Oliver beautifully expresses what is required:

> To live in this world
>
> you must be able
> to do three things:
> to love what is mortal;
> to hold it
>
> against your bones knowing
> your own life depends on it;
> and, when the time comes to let it go,
> to let it go.[8]

Hannah is remarkable in that before she conceived Samuel she had vowed to let him go. Her desire to have a son was not a desire to fulfil her maternal instincts. From the beginning she saw his life as separate from hers. The parting between the mother and the small boy must have been harrowing – but one element one might expect in such a parting was missing. Terrifying though the prospect of separating from her must have been, the child Samuel did not have to cope with his mother's terror on top of his own. She let him go with an exultant expression of confidence in his future. In our dread of letting our children go, we can fail to take into account the possibility that they, too, are afraid and that our fear for them can weigh them down on those critical early steps of their independent journey. We need to remember, as Kahlil Gibran so effectively puts it:

> You are the bows from which your children as living arrows are sent forth.
> The archer sees the mark upon the path of the infinite, and He bends you with His might that His arrows may go swift and far.
> Let your bending in the Archer's hand be for gladness;
> For even as He loves the arrow that flies, so He loves also the bow that is stable.[9]

The parting between Hannah and Samuel is almost unthinkable in a modern context. What parents could contemplate with equanimity the prospect of entrusting a three-year-old to strangers? But the way she handled the parting is an inspiration for any parent today.

The time to let go often arrives without our knowing it. That was the case with Mary and Joseph, when the boy Jesus remained behind them in Jerusalem. This is the only episode of the 'hidden years' of Jesus which is related in Scripture – nothing else of his life is described between his return to Nazareth as a baby after the flight into Egypt, and his emergence into public life thirty years later. We can assume that the incident is therefore of immense importance.

'Child, why have you treated us like this?' Mary asks Jesus, after the three-day search for him ends in the Temple. 'Look, your father and I have been searching for you in great anxiety.' Jesus, in his first recorded words, responds, 'Why were you searching for me? Did you not know that I must be in my Father's house?' (Lk 2:48, 49).

'*Must* be.' Jesus already has a sense of his divine mission, and is conscious that a higher obedience is exacted of him than that due to his earthly parents. Again and again he uses the word 'must' when he speaks of his redemptive mission: 'I must proclaim the good news of the Kingdom of God' (Lk 4:43); 'The Son of man must undergo great suffering' (Lk 9:22); '... so must the Son of man be lifted up' (Jn 3:14); 'I have other sheep that do not belong to this fold; I must bring them also ...' (Jn 10:16).

Immediately after this episode, Jesus returned to Nazareth with Mary and Joseph 'and was obedient to them' (Lk 2:51). For just an instant, we have looked into the future and to an obedience which must always take precedence: the adult Jesus will say, 'Whoever loves father or mother more than me is not worthy of me' (Mt 10:37). In the words of the Episcopal minister and writer, Martin Smith:

> 'He is our peace' ... The gospels, which might have so idealised his relations with his parents, reveal that truth and peace are costly and that there is necessarily pain in the journey from dependence to independence and

through independence to the maturity out of which we
can honour our parents.[10]

Usually, when we pull our children back, it is because we are
frightened for them. When they are little, we know where they
are at all times. It is very hard when that security ends – hard for
us and often hard for them too. Who knows what Jesus felt as a
twelve-year-old boy alone in a large city? Or the homesickness
Samuel experienced after his parents had left Shiloh? What we
can know is what their parents felt, because at some time most
parents will experience the anxiety, the loneliness and the
heartache of a child who has left home for the first time. How
many of us can face this with the strong faith of Hannah? How
many of us can recognise when the time has come to confide our
child with confidence to Gibran's 'house of the future'? Hannah's
triumphant canticle shows how the ending of one story is always
the beginning of another when we willingly became a channel
for God's transformative work. Confidence brought her to the
other side of what Mary Oliver described as 'the black river of
loss' and which transcended desolation:

> Every year
> everything
> I have ever learned
>
> in my lifetime
> leads back to this: the fires
> and the black river of loss
> whose other side
>
> is salvation[11]

Notes

1 RSV.

2 Kahlil Gibran, *The Prophet*, Penguin, 1992, p. 22.

3 David Smail, *Taking Care: An Alternative to Therapy*, London, Robinson, 2001, p. 389.

4 RSV.

5 Smail, op. cit., p. 397.

6 While Hannah is the first to address God directly as 'Lord of hosts', the first use of the term occurs eight verses earlier when, in 1 Sam 1:3, Elkanah is described as going to Shiloh to 'sacrifice to the Lord of hosts'.

7 Kathleen Norris, *Amazing Grace: A Vocabulary of Faith*, New York, Riverhead Books, 1999, p. 107.

8 Mary Oliver, 'In Blackwater Woods', *American Primitive*, USA, Back Bay Books, 1983, p. 82.

9 Kahlil Gibran, op. cit., p. 25.

10 Martin L. Smith, *A Season for the Spirit*, London, Fount, 1991, p. 69.

11 Mary Oliver, op. cit.

6

THE WOMAN WHO WASN'T AFRAID TO LOVE

FORGIVING OURSELVES

My beloved put his hand to the latch,
and my heart was thrilled within me.

Song of Songs 5:4[1]

ENGULFED IN GOD

The great mystic, St Teresa of Avila, said that in the Song of Solomon the Lord is teaching the soul how to pray:

> Along how many paths, in how many ways, by how many methods you show us love! ... in this Song of Songs [you] teach the soul what to say to you ... We can make the Bride's prayer our own.[2]

When I first read these words of Teresa's, I revisited the Song of Solomon and chose a passage at random as a form of prayer:

> As the apple tree among the trees of the wood,
> so is my beloved among the sons.
> With great delight I sat in his shadow,
> and his fruit was sweet to my taste.

He brought me to the banqueting house,
and his intention towards me was love.
Sustain me with raisins,
refresh me with apples;
for I am faint with love.
Oh that his left hand were under my head.
and that his right hand embraced me! (Song 2:3-6)

My reaction to the experience of *praying* the Song of Solomon was a revelation to me. I have to say it felt completely alien – almost shocking in its loving, desiring, tactile imagery. If Teresa was right and this is the kind of language in which God longs to hear the soul speak, it seemed to me that I had to make a radical shift in my perception of what it is to love and be loved by God. Up to then, I had thought of ecstatic delight in God's presence as the preserve of mystics, inaccessible to people living among the commonplace realities of everyday life. Prayer as passionate seeking, as desolation in the absence of the beloved, and rapture in finding him – this kind of prayer was utterly outside my experience. It felt unnatural, irreverent. I could not imagine myself experiencing prayer as described by Teresa:

> I used unexpectedly to experience a consciousness of the presence of God of such a kind that I could not possibly doubt that he was within me or that I was wholly engulfed in him.[3]

In the parable of the rich man and Lazarus I have often felt like the former. When he died, the rich man could see 'Abraham, far off' but between both there existed a great chasm which could not be bridged. In the same way, God can seem very far off – perceived but not experienced. The chasm separating us from him is often the past. Past failures can take unrelenting possession of us. We can become haunted by the memory of bad decisions, missed opportunities, unrealised potential. The sense of steps taken irretrievably in the wrong direction, of having done irreparable harm, can be crippling – attaching to our spirit like a leech, draining us of hope and optimism, so that – in Donne's powerful line – 'I am rebegot/Of absence, darkness, death; things which are not'.[4]

This terrifying awareness of repeated failure creates a malign force field which sucks our energies inward. We make half-hearted efforts to move forward, but then think 'too little, too late' and retreat into our inadequacy. We dig a hole, put our talent into it, and pile the stifling earth on top. 'I was afraid, and I went and hid your talent in the ground' (Mt 25:25). The parable of the ten talents reminds us that nothing can excuse inaction. We must spend our lives with an energy which has nothing to do with what we consider our worth to be. The fact that we may have fallen again and again on our life's journey does not permit us to pause, let alone stop altogether. The fact that we have failed ourselves and failed others does not excuse us from a continual effort to forgive and love – and that process starts with ourselves. If we cannot accept that we ourselves are forgiven, we cannot forgive others. If we cannot weep for ourselves, how can we 'weep with those who weep' (Rom 12:15)?

In the Eastern Orthodox Church, the services held from Sunday through Tuesday evening of Holy Week are called the

'Bridegroom Services' because the central theme is 'Behold, the Bridegroom Comes'. The Christ of the Passion is the Christ who is moving towards union with the beloved. He is also the Christ of the Second Coming, for whom we must be ready and prepared. Towards the end of the Tuesday evening Bridegroom Service the extraordinarily beautiful Hymn of Kassiani is sung. Composed by a ninth-century Byzantine abbess, one of the earliest known women composers, the hymn tells of the woman who washed Christ's feet in the house of Simon the Pharisee. This woman does not speak in the Gospel accounts, but Kassiani imagines her thoughts as she pours myrrh on the feet of Jesus. It begins:

> O Lord, the woman who had fallen into many sins,
> perceiving Your divinity,
> took the part of a myrrh-bearer;
> weeping, she brings oils of myrrh
> before your burial.

> 'Woe to me,' she says, 'for night
> is a frenzy of lust to me,
> a dark, moonless love of sin.'

The unaccompanied chant resonates through the dimly lit church, dipping and soaring in great plangent waves of sound, nuanced and passionate. It is one of the great hymns of the Eastern Church; the Greek-Canadian composer Christos Hatzis said of it:

> It literally bursts at the seams with emotion and feminine energy. Kassiani's Magdalen[5] constantly

bounces between the depths of despair and the heights of spiritual passion. Utter darkness and cosmic majesty are depicted often in a single sentence and there is a passionate pleading for mercy and an intense spiritual devotion that borders on the erotic.[6]

THE UNWELCOME GUESTS

This woman, described in Luke 7, breaks upon an uncomfortable scene. Jesus is being entertained at the house of Simon the Pharisee, who has welcomed him with minimal hospitality – indeed, his omission of the common courtesies of the time amounts to a calculated insult. There is no kiss of greeting; no offer is made to wash the dust of the road from the guest's feet; there is no anointing of the head with oil. What is behind Simon's invitation, that he receives Jesus in a way that is so guarded, if not openly hostile? Perhaps curiosity, or perhaps a desire to interrogate Jesus and test his orthodoxy – we are not told.

Many people will have had the experience of being, at some time or another, an unwelcome guest – responding to an invitation which the giver feels bound to give and which the recipient feels obliged to accept. Then comes the ordeal of the event, the invitee conscious of the host's disapproval or wariness, the polite, brittle conversation and the overwhelming relief when the whole thing is over.

Into this unfriendly environment comes someone who is even less welcome:

> And a woman in the city, who was a sinner, having learned that he was eating in the Pharisee's house, brought an alabaster flask of ointment. She stood behind

> him at his feet, weeping, and began to bathe his feet with her tears and to dry them with her hair. Then she continued kissing his feet and anointing them with the ointment. (Lk 7:37-38)

It is a marvellous incident. This woman *accepted* that she had been forgiven. It is likely she has already met Jesus – perhaps she was among the crowd at Capernaum when Jesus said, 'Everything that the Father gives me will come to me; and anyone who comes to me I will never drive away' (Jn 6:37). It is *because* she is forgiven that she shows such love to Jesus: 'Therefore, I tell you, her sins, which were many, have been forgiven; hence she has shown great love.' (Lk 7:47)

Translations of this verse can also read, 'her sins have been forgiven because she loved much'. Biblical scholars have argued over whether the forgiveness occurred before or as a result of the meeting in Simon's house. It seems to me that the former makes more sense: her love followed her forgiveness. The significance of this is that accepting that she was forgiven made it possible for the woman to show such love.

A prostitute was regarded as unclean. To be touched by her was to become unclean. Simon regarded Jesus' reaction to the woman's caresses as clear evidence that he was no prophet: 'He said to himself, "If this man were a prophet, he would have known who and what sort of woman this is who is touching him, for she is a sinner".'

The woman never speaks; her love and repentance are beyond words. This is the most sensual scene in the New Testament – the erotic overtones of the cascade of hair (in ancient Israel only prostitutes wore their hair loose in public), the perfumed air, the smoothing on of the aromatic ointment, the woman's lips pressed over and over again on Christ's bare feet. He accepts her touch as fitting and right; he welcomes her unconscious intimacy, sees beyond her reputation and her behaviour and into her heart.

Where Simon sees rank sexuality, Jesus sees love. This unspeaking woman is praying with her body and with her heart. It is a way we seldom pray. Her prayer is part of a tradition as old as the passionate, lyrical and sensuous Song of Solomon. God delights in every aspect of his creation – physical as well as spiritual. It was into our *bodies* that he breathed the spirit of life. It is through our bodies that we make the journey towards him. Over and over in Scripture, his love for his people is expressed in highly tactile imagery – the cradling of an infant in its mother's arms, the dandling of a toddler on its father's knee, the love of a bridegroom and a bride.

THE TERROR OF UNCONDITIONAL LOVE

It isn't difficult to imagine the woman in Simon's house praying the Song of Solomon. 'How much better is your love than wine! The fragrance of your perfumes than all manner of spices!' (Song 1:2)[7] As Teresa of Avila wrote, 'it is not a matter of thinking much, but of loving much'. Reading Simon's thoughts, Jesus asks him to consider a scenario in which a creditor forgives two debtors. Which debtor would be more grateful and loving, he asks, the one who was forgiven the greater or lesser debt?

> Then turning toward the woman, he said to Simon, 'Do you see this woman? I entered your house; you gave me no water for my feet, but she has bathed my feet with

her tears and dried them with her hair. You gave me no kiss, but from the time I came in she has not stopped kissing my feet. You did not anoint my head with oil, but she has anointed my feet with ointment. Therefore, I tell you, her sins, which were many, have been forgiven; hence she has shown great love. But the one to whom little is forgiven, loves little.' (Lk 7:44-47)

I suspect that there is a lot more of Simon in many of us than there is of the unnamed woman. His belief system is so neatly defined and has such precise limits. True religion to him is confining rather than liberating. It is a constraint rather than a driving force, authoritarian rather than authoritative. It is a belief system in which 'observance' is everything and in which everything is measured. Simon 'observes' the law, without appreciating its true function: to channel the mercy of God to mankind. Jesus, the very manifestation of God's mercy, is there at Simon's table and Simon cannot see it. Simon's house was a place in which sinners were best kept out rather than embraced. His niggardly reception of Jesus is in extreme contrast to the extravagance shown by the woman. The ointment which she pours so freely over Jesus' feet was probably spikenard, a jar of which, in the time of Jesus, cost around 300 denarii – a year's wages for a labourer. A few days earlier, speaking to the multitude at the Sermon on the Mount, Jesus had said: 'Forgive, and you will be forgiven; give, and it will be given to you. A good measure, pressed down, shaken together, running over, will be put into your lap.' (Lk 6:37, 38)

It may be hard to forgive, but it can be harder to ask for and accept forgiveness. The ability to believe we are forgiven is crucial to our spiritual growth. This was the defining difference between Peter and Judas. Vacillating Peter went from the shame of his threefold denial of Christ to become the rock on which Christ's church was founded. Judas could not contemplate the possibility of forgiveness. He, who had heard Christ say that one must forgive seventy times seven, could not bring himself to ask Christ to forgive him. Instead, he died in despair. It is easy to forget the other side of the coin – if we must be prepared to forgive seventy times seven, then we must also be ready to ask for forgiveness – and believe we are forgiven – seventy times seven.

Self-loathing leads inevitably to despair. Thomas Merton describes the process:

> Despair is the ultimate development of a pride so great and so stiff-necked that it selects the absolute misery of damnation rather than accept happiness from the hands of God and thereby acknowledge that He is above us and that we are not capable of fulfilling our destiny by ourselves.[8]

The unnamed woman in Simon's house knew what Eve did not. Unlike Eve, she did not hide, but approached Jesus with the confidence of love, knowing that God's mercy and compassion were greater than her sins. In Kassiani's words:

> I shall kiss your immaculate feet,
> wipe them again with the hair of my head,
> those feet at whose sound Eve in Paradise
> in the cool of the day, hid for fear.

A very short time after this episode, Jesus will himself wash his disciples' feet, in a similar act of love and humility. Just as we can find it hard to accept forgiveness and love, Peter, at the Last Supper, was horrified at the notion of Jesus stooping to wash his feet. He overcame this reluctance, but it was after this incident that Judas left in disgust. In Martin Smith's spiritual classic, *A Season for the Spirit*, he summarises the significance of this episode:

> The foot washing throws light on how the Cross judges us. The issue is whether we will accept absolute and unconditional love and allow it to envelop and penetrate us wholly. Judas' disgust with [Jesus] becomes total and he goes out into the night to betray him. The mystery of damnation is the possibility deep in the heart of every human being of totally repudiating the embrace of Divine Love in a final 'No'.[9]

Peter has to overcome his repugnance at the idea of Jesus stooping to wash his feet. Jesus kneels at *our* feet, as he did at Peter's, and he addresses the same words to us: 'Unless I wash you, you have no share with me.' (Jn 13:8) But have I the courage and the generosity to accept his forgiveness and unconditional love?

FORGIVENESS IS SELDOM EARNED

The faults we most dislike in others are our own faults. The weaknesses we most despise in others are our own weaknesses. If we are devoured by self-loathing for our failings, how can we forgive these failings in others? If we cannot love ourselves when we fall, how can we love others in their falling? It is easier to hold back like Simon than to see ourselves as we really are, in all our vulnerability, and to lay our cheek against the feet of Christ. If we are angry, bitter, cynical, it is often because there is something in our heart for which we have not forgiven ourselves, someone else, or indeed God. Simon, like many people, insulates himself from what he is by rigid observance of a code of conduct. He concentrates on earning rather than receiving. He risks nothing, and he never experiences surrender.

Simon is a bit like the elder brother in the parable of the Prodigal Son – another character with whom is it easy to identify. We can empathise with his outrage at the fuss made over the return of his profligate brother. The elder brother believed that he *deserved* his place in his father's house. The Anglican theologian Harry Williams elaborates on this:

> The older brother looked for something earned, for the wages which are paid in families under one euphemism or another. He looked for something earned and was confronted with something spontaneously given for the sheer joy of it. And his moral universe was undermined ... The prodigal was given no opportunity for dwelling on his wickedness ... For that would have been for him to seek security in his own poor estimate of himself rather than in his father's irrepressible love. And when the time came, he found that ... all he could do was to receive.[10]

Forgiveness is rarely *deserved*. If we rejoice in knowing ourselves forgiven despite our unworthiness, we will be much more ready to forgive others. If there is tension in a relationship, our instinct is to avoid it. If we have injured someone, it is often easier to hide than to ask for forgiveness – like Eve in Paradise 'in the cool of the day'. We tend to stay away from that person until the issue is resolved. But the longer we stay away, the less likely a resolution becomes. And if the conflict is within ourselves, rather than with someone else, we may end up growing a carapace over the wound and living life on the surface rather than with our whole being. Like Simon, we adhere to a familiar code of behaviour which leaves our interior landscape a desert in which the clouds of dust prevent our seeing that the source of all life and love is as close to us as a guest at our own table.

In the story of the paralytic whose friends cut a hole in the roof to get him before Jesus, I have at times of my life identified closely with the paralytic. It seemed to me that I had walked away from God, and the farther I walked the weaker I became. Finally, I had no strength to turn and walk back. I was paralysed spiritually – so drained by apathy and discouragement that it seemed impossible to turn towards God for healing. There are times when we need to be helped to ask for healing, or to help others to do so. It was the faith of his friends and not the paralysed man's own faith to which Jesus responded: 'And when Jesus saw their faith, he said to the paralytic, "Son, your sons are forgiven".' (Mk 2:5) Jesus in his act of healing looked at the whole person. He recognised that the man's paralysis was not just physical.

When we forgive, and when we are forgiven, a crippling burden is lifted from our shoulders. We can then, like the man in this episode, rise and walk. Christ is always there to help us lift this weight. The possibility is always there for us to turn to him and let him heal us – so that, along with the crowd that witnessed the healing of the paralytic, we can exclaim, 'We have never seen anything like this!' (Mk 2:12) We can hear the words of Psalm 103 with our hearts, rather than with our ears:

> The Lord is merciful and gracious,
> slow to anger, and abounding in steadfast love.
> He will not always accuse,
> nor will he keep his anger for ever.
> He does not deal with us according to our sins,
> nor repay us according to our iniquities.
> For as high as the heavens are high above the earth,
> so great is his steadfast love for those who fear him;
> as far as the east is from the west,
> so far has he removed our transgressions from us.
> (Ps 103:8-12)

There is an old story which describes Peter at the gates of heaven. The world has ended. The sheep have been separated from the goats; all the faithful have entered heaven and Peter is preparing to close the gates. Then he sees Jesus standing outside. 'Master,' he says, 'what are you doing outside?' Jesus replies, 'I'm waiting for Judas.'

Jesus will wait for me, too, beyond the end of time. But I can only go to him within time. And he cannot force me to go to him. He stands at the door and knocks. The reaction he wants is that of the bride in the Song of Solomon:

My beloved put his hand to the latch,
and my heart was thrilled within me.
I arose to open to my beloved,
and my hands dripped with myrrh,
my fingers with liquid myrrh,
upon the handles of the bolt. (Song 5:4-5)[11]

NOTES

1 RSV.

2 St Teresa of Avila, *Conceptions of the Love of God*, London and New York, Burns & Oates, 2002, p. 380, 382.

3 E. Allison Peers (translator), *The Life of St Teresa of Avila*, New York, Doubleday Books, 1960, p. 119.

4 John Donne, 'A Nocturnall upon S. Lucies Day', in H.J.C. Grierson (ed.), *Metaphysical Lyrics and Poems of the Seventeenth Century*, Oxford University Press, 1971, p. 13.

5 Often referred to as Mary Magdalen, the woman in the story narrated by Luke in Chapter 7 of his gospel is actually unnamed.

6 Christos Hatzis quoted in an article by Brendan McCarthy, 'A Woman of Byzantium', *The Tablet*, 28 February 2004, accessed at *The Tablet* website: www.thetablet.co.uk.

7 *New American Standard Bible* (NASB).

8 Thomas Merton, *New Seeds of Contemplation*, Boston, Shambhala Publications, 2003, p. 180.

9 Martin L. Smith, *A Season for the Spirit*, London, Fount, 1991, p. 152.

10 H.A. Williams, *The True Wilderness*, London, Constable, 1965, pp. 78–9.

11 RSV.

WRESTLING WITH GOD

Jacob at the Jabbok

What we choose to fight is so tiny!
What fights with us is so great!

Rainer Maria Rilke, 'The Man Watching'

A VERY CONTEMPORARY BATTLEFIELD

One of the most haunting episodes in Genesis is the wordless night-long wrestle between Jacob and the mysterious figure at the ford of the Jabbok, on the north-eastern frontier of the Promised Land. The eerie battlefield on the banks of the Jabbok is universal. Somewhere along our journey, most of us will find ourselves there. As with Jacob, there comes a time when, in order to go forward, we must first stop. We have to stand back from everybody and every thing in our lives and – utterly alone with ourselves – confront all the compromises we have made. In order to find our way, we have to go deep into the trackless dark. We have to grapple with our demons and our angels and pray to the invisible God that the angels will win. To me, this prayer found its supreme expression in a sonnet written by John Donne (himself no stranger to compromise) four hundred years ago:

> Batter my heart, three personed God; for, you
> As yet but knock, breathe, shine, and seek to mend;
> That I may rise, and stand, o'erthrow me, and bend
> Your force, to break, blow, burn and make me new.

Donne unforgettably describes his soul as a city occupied by an enemy, but desperately trying to admit God, 'Yet dearly I love you, and would be loved faine/But am betroth'd unto your enemy'. The sonnet reaches its climax in the passionate plea:

> Take me to you, imprison me, for I
> Except you enthral me, never shall be free,
> Nor ever chaste, except you ravish me.[1]

The Bible has always been a rich source of inspiration for artists. It is interesting and surprising to note that this dramatic incident in the life of Jacob was largely neglected until relatively modern times. Apart from one painting by Rembrandt and one by Claude Lorraine, the theme failed to capture the artistic imagination until the nineteenth century when the great Romantic artist, Eugene Delacroix, painted his magnificent fresco, 'Jacob Wrestling the Angel', on the walls of St Sulpice in Paris. It was the artist's last major work and has been described as his 'spiritual testament'. The Symbolist artists, who were greatly influenced by Delacroix, embraced the theme enthusiastically – Moreau and Redon painted it; Paul Gauguin used it for his first masterpiece, 'Vision after the Sermon'. Twentieth-century poets Rainer Maria Rilke and Gerard Manley Hopkins seized upon the Jacob story, along with writers as diverse as August Strindberg, André Malraux and Roland Barthes. Twentieth-century painters who continued to address the theme include Marc Chagall, Jacob Kainen and Hananiah Harari. In sculpture, Tate Britain has a stunning seven-foot-high 'Jacob and the Angel', carved by Jacob Epstein in the middle of World War II.

Why should this strange story touch a modern nerve so strongly? I believe it is because Jacob – perhaps more than anyone else in the Bible – is Everyman. That silent, gruelling struggle with God, the search for identity and wholeness, and the hunger to be blessed, are preoccupations as relevant today as they were four thousand years ago. More relevant than ever, too, is the desire for position and status. Rabbi Harold Kushner sums it up when he writes about Jacob: 'We need to know that we matter to the world, that the world takes us seriously ... at the same time, we need to be assured that we are good people.'[2] There are times in each of our lives when we face a crisis, in the original meaning of the Greek word as 'turning point' – described by Ivan Illich as 'the instant of choice, that marvellous moment when people suddenly become aware of their self-imposed cages, and of the possibility of a different life'.[3] When I experienced such a crisis in my own life, I turned to the story of Jacob and his nocturnal conflict and found it fiercely illuminating.

THE FLAWED PATRIARCH

The patriarch of the twelve tribes of Israel was – like so many biblical characters – deeply flawed. The younger son of Isaac and Rebekah, Jacob's name means 'he who supplants' or 'he who grabs the heel'. His life was one of restless ambition from his conception. He and his older twin brother Esau 'struggled together' in their mother's womb. When Esau was born, Jacob followed, grabbing his brother fast by the heel. The spoiled son of a doting mother, Jacob ruthlessly deceived his blind old father and cheated his brother Esau out of the inheritance and blessing due to him as the eldest son. Dressed in Esau's clothes, and with hairy skins attached to his arms and chest, Jacob the 'smooth man' successfully passed himself off as his hirsute brother and secured Isaac's blessing. Jacob had to flee Esau's understandable rage, and he sought refuge with his mother's brother Laban in far off Mesopotamia.

He travelled with few possessions and slept under the stars. At Bethel, north of Jerusalem, when he seemed utterly destitute, he lay with his head on a stone and dreamed that a ladder led from that spot to the highest heavens, with angels ascending and descending on it. '... the air a staircase/For silence/... all that close throng/Of spirits waiting, as I/For the message.'[4] In the dream, God promised that he would give to Jacob and his descendants the land on which he lay, 'and you shall spread abroad to the west and to the east and to the north and to the south; and by you and your descendants shall all the families of the earth bless themselves' (Gen 28:14).

When Jacob awoke, he exclaimed 'How awesome is this place! This is none other than the house of God, and this is the gate of heaven!' (Gen 28:17) He swore that he would raise a temple to the Lord on this spot when the Lord's promise was fulfilled and when he would be in a position to return in peace to his father's house. The realisation of this promise must have seemed very remote as Jacob arrived at his uncle's house and began a long period of voluntary servitude. In his wily uncle, he met his match for sharp practice. The twenty years that followed were filled with trickery on both sides. Jacob fell in love with Laban's daughter Rachel and served his uncle seven years to win her hand, 'and they seemed to him but a few days because of the love he had for her'. However, when the long awaited wedding day arrived, Laban substituted his elder daughter Leah for Rachel. When Jacob realised he had been duped, Laban told him, 'it is not done in our country to give the younger before the firstborn' (Gen 29:26). One can only imagine the feelings of the man who had usurped the position of his own older sibling! Laban then agreed to let him marry Rachel as well, but demanded another seven years' labour in return. Only after fourteen years could Jacob start earning and it took six years for him to earn enough to become independent.

At last, Jacob felt secure. He had wives, children, flocks. The man who crossed the Jordan with only his staff had become a man of considerable substance. He decided to return to the land of his birth. Jacob evidently believed that his hard-won status would enable him to face Esau again and would allow him to buy his brother's forgiveness. What he did not yet realise was that, in terms of moral courage, he was destitute.

Laban did not welcome the news of Jacob's imminent departure, and some more double-crossing ensued between uncle and nephew. During this time, God encouraged Jacob to follow through on his decision, urging him to 'go forth from this land and return to the land of your birth'. Finally, Jacob succeeded in extricating himself, his family and all his belongings (including, typically, some that were not his) from Laban's grasp. His furious uncle came in hot pursuit. Laban overtook his nephew in Gilead but was ordered by God to refrain from harming him. After being reconciled with Laban, Jacob continued on his way with his wives, children and flocks, finally arriving at the river Jabbok in the Transjordan.

The Jabbok rises in Amman and runs a course of about sixty-five miles through a wild and deep ravine before joining the Jordan river between Gennesaret and the Dead Sea. It formed one of the boundaries of ancient Israel. In its course, it drops steeply from 2,700 feet above sea level to 1,000 feet below sea level. As Jacob approached the frontier, his courage, like the river, plummeted. He began to summon up his resources for the inevitable encounter with Esau. Camping on the river bank, he sent messengers ahead of him to the brother whom he wronged:

> Thus shall you say to my lord Esau, Thus says your servant Jacob: 'I have lived with Laban as an alien and stayed until now; and I have oxen, donkeys, flocks, male and female servants; and I have sent to tell my lord, in order that I may find favour in your sight.' (Gen 32:4, 5)

The messengers returned to Jacob with very unwelcome news: 'We came to your brother Esau, and he is coming to meet you and four hundred men are with him.' Jacob was 'greatly afraid and distressed' and prayed to God for deliverance: 'Deliver me, please, from the hand of my brother, from the hand of Esau, for I am afraid of him; he may come and kill us all, the mothers with their children.' (Gen 32:11) He divided his company into two groups, thinking, 'If Esau comes to one company and destroys it, then the company that is left will escape.'

He then sent several droves of livestock across the river to Esau:

He instructed the foremost, 'When Esau my brother meets you, and asks you, "To whom do you belong? Where are you going? And whose are these ahead of you?" then you shall say, "They belong to your servant Jacob; they are a present sent to my lord Esau; and moreover he is behind us."' He likewise instructed the second and the third and all who followed the droves, 'You shall say the same thing to Esau when you meet him, and you shall say, "Moreover your servant Jacob is behind us."' For he thought, 'I may appease him with the present that goes ahead of me, and afterwards I shall see his face; perhaps he will accept me'. (Gen 32:17-20)

SELF-KNOWLEDGE: ANGELS AND DEMONS

Having done this, Jacob crossed the Jabbok with his two wives and their eleven children and sent them on ahead. He remained alone by the river as night fell. Into this dark and brooding atmosphere a stranger came, and launched a violent attack on Jacob. Jacob reacted quickly and powerfully to the assault. The ensuing struggle was gruelling; the opponents fought each other to the limits of endurance. There were no weapons, just body grappling with body hour after hour in a brutal, wordless encounter. While the world slept, Jacob fought for his survival, unable even to see the face of his adversary. As dawn crept over the horizon, and Jacob was bracing himself for what must have seemed the thousandth effort, he was suddenly disabled. His unseen opponent had effortlessly dislocated Jacob's thigh.

It was at this point that the first words were spoken. Jacob's opponent said, 'Let me go, for the day is breaking'. It is a measure of Jacob's tenacity that, crippled by pain as he must have been, he could still grip the stranger so powerfully that he had to ask Jacob to release him. It is also extraordinary that someone who had the power to disable Jacob with a touch should still have to beg to be released. 'I will not let you go,' Jacob said between clenched teeth, 'unless you bless me'. Having battled so long and hard with his antagonist, giving as good as he got, Jacob knew that no human hand could have disabled him with a mere touch. He had not been fighting with a mortal, but with a manifestation of God (described as an 'angel' in Hosea 12:4). Having prevailed in equal contest, duplicitous Jacob was himself cheated – the victory which should have been his was usurped by a supernatural touch.

Before he would bless Jacob, the angel forced a confession from him. 'What is your name?' he asked. And Jacob was forced into admitting, 'I am Jacob'. In ancient narrative, one's personality and one's very self were inextricably linked with one's name; a name held a person's destiny. In giving his name, Jacob was confessing to everything that has marked his life to date: 'I am the one who supplants; the one who grasps what is not his, the one who deceives.' In Gen 27:36, Esau cried out, 'Is he not rightly named Jacob? For he has supplanted me these two times. He took away my birthright; and behold, now he has taken away my blessing'.

Motifs from the past emerge in the combat. Jacob, the heel grabber, who refused to let his brother go at birth and who grasped everything he wanted thereafter, clung with the same tenacity to his supernatural opponent. Jacob, who went to his blind father disguised as his brother and swindled Esau out of his rightful inheritance, now had to admit his true, flawed identity to an opponent whom he could not see before he could receive a blessing. Without this admission, this self-knowledge, Jacob could not be blessed. Without the closeness of the hand-to-hand combat, he could not be blessed. Jacob, the arch compromiser, could not keep God or his own true self at a distance, and still expect to be blessed.

'Noverim me, noverim te', prayed St Thomas Aquinas. 'Let me know myself, so that I may know you.' 'Who are you?', the angel asked Jacob, and Jacob in turn put the same question to the angel. God is the answer; God is the question.

The fight was a cathartic experience. Jacob had always relied on his wits to get what he wanted and to extricate himself from undesirable situations. A master of the oblique, he had avoided direct confrontation. His life had been marked by elaborate deceptions perpetrated both by him and upon him. His is a story of names and identities stolen and hidden; disguises adopted; and a blessing obtained by deceit. I am sure I am not alone in finding it all too easy to identify with many aspects of this biblical anti-hero's character. I take a lot of comfort from the way in which he rose to God's challenge despite all his flaws. On the banks of the Jabbok, God forced him into a face-to-face confrontation and Jacob found he had resources he didn't know he possessed. In hand-to-hand fighting there is no room for pretence, for ambiguity, no room to hide. Jacob's refusal to be crushed by his own defects is the key to his greatness. I imagine he would have had no difficulty with the message of the Parable of the Talents. He displayed courage, endurance, tenacity and – when he was unfairly immobilised – he conceded only on his own terms.

Jacob's determination was rewarded in a most liberating way, and one which can give us confidence when we feel crippled by our own personality. When he admitted his name, the response was immediate. 'You shall no longer be called Jacob, but Israel [literally 'he who strives with God'], for you have striven with God and with humans, and have prevailed.' As with other biblical figures (Abram/Abraham, Simon/Peter, Saul/Paul), a change of name indicated a new beginning. 'Who are you?' 'Jacob.' By renaming him, God is saying 'No, you are more than you think you are.' Jacob in turn asked: 'Please tell me your name.' He replied, 'Why is it you ask my name?' With that, he blessed him there. Jacob named the place Peniel, 'Because I have seen God face to face,' he said, 'and have survived.'

The sun rose as he passed Peniel, limping from his hip (Gen 32:29-31). To quote again from Rabbi Harold Kushner on Jacob:

> It hurts to be defeated by conscience, to feel compelled to take the more demanding high road, to resist temptation, to apologise ... it hurts more to keep winning out over conscience ... When the struggle is over we will, like Jacob, be bruised and limping. But ... we will be at peace with ourselves in a way we never were before.[5]

Jacob had pleaded with God to deliver him from the wrath of Esau. Now came the answer to his prayer – his discovery of his own strength, a strength grounded in self-knowledge. There would be no miraculous intervention to protect him from Esau. With the courage Jacob found in the nocturnal encounter, and with this alone, he went out to meet his brother. The answer to prayer is often already in our possession, but, like Jacob, we may not realise it. The moment he had dreaded so much arrived:

> Now Jacob looked up and saw Esau coming and four hundred men with him. So he divided the children among Leah and Rachel and the two maids. He put the maids with their children in front, then Leah with her children, and Rachel and Joseph last of all. He himself went on ahead of them, bowing himself to the ground seven times, until he came near his brother. But Esau ran to meet him, took him in his arms, threw himself on his neck and wept as he kissed him ... Jacob said to him ... 'Truly to see your face is like seeing the face of God'. (Gen 33:1-4, 10)

Even in the context of meeting a brother whom he has wronged, Jacob's statement is arresting. It casts a great deal of light on the mysterious wrestling episode. It is evident that in the brother whom he injured and who now forgave him, Jacob sees the face of the same Person with whom he struggled through the night. Jacob has been wrestling with his own angels and demons, with the deceptions which have, over time, fragmented his identity. He has been battling his past and especially the cruel hoax he perpetrated on his father and brother. St Gregory the Great understands Jacob in this story as representing all those who pray. Fully aware of Jacob's defects, Gregory also recognises Jacob's unquenchable desire to move forward, always craving a blessing, as a decisive factor in his life. He describes it as an example of the long and gradual spiritual ascent of the human soul, detaching itself from falsehood and becoming more and more familiar with true reality.[6]

What was Jacob fighting? There is a large painting of Jacob wrestling by the French Symbolist painter Gustave Moreau in Harvard's Fogg Art Museum. In it, Jacob is vigorously straining against thin air. His expression is fiercely concentrated; every sinew in his body is stretched. The angel – serene and compassionate – is standing to one side, unseen by Jacob.

The battlefield is within Jacob, as it is within all of us. He has been in thrall to power, position, possessions. To achieve them, he has almost sold his soul. Now he has come to this isolated place, and has sent all his family and all his possessions into Canaan. When he himself enters his homeland he will be faced with the actuality of his wrongdoing so many years before. The confrontation with Esau will make or break him. He has nerved himself to this point, but now he has to make an even more perilous interior journey. Decades of duplicity, acquisitiveness and compromise have fractured his personality. He has to forge integrity out of disintegration. The self-deception he has practised has become so much a part of him that to excise it will take extraordinary effort and courage.

In the wrestling match and its conclusion, a remarkable thing had happened. The boundaries between Jacob and the angel became blurred. The balance of power shifted back and forth; the weaker prevailed over the stronger; the stronger, despite supernatural powers, had to beg to be released by the weaker. The weaker, although forcing the stronger to bless him, was lastingly wounded – perhaps as much by his own past treacheries as by God. Identities were hidden, revealed, guessed at. The angel took on some of Jacob's weakness and Jacob some of the angel's strength. Mortal Jacob wrestled with the Eternal; from Jacob's seed will spring the One who is and was and is to come. And we need to remember that while Jacob was attacked by the angel, Jacob chose the battlefield. He didn't need to remain alone in that isolated and sinister spot as night thickened around him. As a demonstration of God being in us, as we are in God, this episode is unparallelled.

CRISIS AS TURNING POINT

Nobody looks forward to this kind of crisis, but if it becomes unavoidable we can at least approach it as the positive experience Ivan Illich described. For many of us there will come a day when we realise that our journey has ground to a halt and that we have to fight whatever it is that is holding us back. It may be an undesirable pattern of behaviour, an addiction, major difficulty in a relationship, the bitterness of an old resentment, greed, envy, fear or a range of other things hanging like millstones around our necks. Whatever our particular millstone is, we will almost always try to mask its presence to others and to ourselves; and it will always be an impediment to loving. If we refuse to see what is draining the love and energy out of us, then we are living a lie. When, at last, the weight of the millstone becomes too great we can chose whether to sit down under its weight, or try to remove it. It may seem to us that the thing we are trying to fight is too strong for us; our particular millstone has fused so closely with us that, even if we succeeded in excising it, we feel we would be mortally wounded. It is one of the starkest decisions we will have to make. Søren Kierkegaard describes it perfectly:

Do you not know that there comes a midnight hour when every one has to throw off his mask? Do you believe that life will always let itself be mocked? Do you think you can slip away a little before midnight in order to avoid this? Or are you not terrified by it? I have seen men in real life who so long deceived others that at last their true nature could not reveal itself ... In every man there is something which to a certain degree prevents him from becoming perfectly transparent to himself; and this may be the case in so high a degree, he may be so inexplicably woven into relationships of life which extend far beyond himself that he almost cannot reveal himself. But he who cannot reveal himself cannot love, and he who cannot love is the most unhappy man of all.[7]

Jacob, physically damaged but morally strengthened, limped away from the Jabbok to begin a new phase of his journey – no longer as Jacob but as Israel. Boundaries continued to shift in this extraordinary story. When the sun came up, Jacob had prevailed, but he still had not seen the face of his opponent. When that face was revealed, it was the face of God but at the same time it was the face of his dreaded brother: Jacob said to Esau, 'Truly to see your face is like seeing the face of God'. The displaced and vengeful older brother had taken on the characteristics of a forgiving father. Jacob, seeing his wronged brother coming, bowed repeatedly to the ground. 'But Esau ran to meet him, and embraced him, and fell on his neck and kissed him, and they wept.'

Was Jesus remembering this incident when he told the story of the Prodigal Son? 'While he was far off, his father saw him and was filled with compassion. He ran and put his arm around him and kissed him.' (Lk 15:20) Jacob is like the Prodigal's older brother, whose concept of forgiveness is that of something that has to be earned rather than freely given and accepted. Having stripped Esau of his birthright so many years before, Jacob was desperate to make amends. He pressed his gifts upon Esau, who replied, 'I have enough, my brother; keep what you have for yourself'.

Jacob's cold formality contrasts with Esau's wholehearted pardon. Just as it can be easier to identify with the icily virtuous Pharisee, Simon, than with the forgiven woman who showed her love for Jesus so extravagantly, so it is the case with Jacob and Esau. Jacob came prepared to make abundant amends and so win his brother's forgiveness. He was disconcerted by the generosity of Esau's reception and, Jacob-like, would not rest until he had forced Esau to accept his gifts. After that, he couldn't wait to get away from his brother. Esau assumed that Jacob was coming to his home at Seir – perhaps Isaac, very old by now, was living with him there. He courteously offered to accompany Jacob on the journey, but Jacob declined his offer. Esau then urged him to accept at least an escort, which Jacob also declined – making the excuse that his children and cattle needed to travel slowly. 'I will go on slowly, according to the pace of the cattle that are before me and according to the pace of the children, until I come to my lord in Seir.'

As soon as Esau was out of sight, Jacob, instead of following him south to Seir, headed in the opposite direction, to Succoth, north-west of Peniel where the brothers had met. Not only was he deceiving Esau yet again, but he was delaying his response to

God's command to return to the land of his birth, and his own promise to return to Bethel and built an altar there. This was no temporary diversion, since we are told that Jacob built himself a house in Succoth and outhouses for his livestock. He was clearly planning a prolonged stay.

It is so easy to identify with Jacob. It happens so often that we pray desperately for something and then, when we receive it, we become complacent. In our periods of anxiety or terror, we rush to God, wrestling with him in prayer. When the crisis recedes, we recover confidence in our ability to work things out ourselves. Spiritually, we are safest in times of great danger; it is when we feel safe that we are spiritually extremely vulnerable. And so Jacob, having survived the dreaded encounter with Esau, decides he will take his time about engaging further. Without compunction, he heads off in another direction, leaving Esau to wait in Seir for a brother who was not going to arrive. It is an odd way for a man who claimed to see 'the face of God' in his forgiving brother to behave. But then, we all behave in odd ways towards the God who forgives us. How many times has God been moved with pity for us in our weakness? How many times has he opened his arms and embraced us on life's journey? Each time, he invites us to travel with him to our destination, our Seir, but how easy it is to take some lengthy detours instead! How easy it is to say, like Jacob, 'There's no need to stay with me – I'll follow at my own pace'. And, like Jacob, there are times when instead of following, we actually turn back. The problem is that it is very hard to worship God in the place where we are not supposed to be.

It is interesting to note that when Abram and Saul become Abraham and Paul, they are never thereafter called by their old names. After he renames Simon as Peter 'the rock', Jesus still occasionally calls him by his old name, usually when he fails to live up to the new one: 'Simon, Simon, listen! Satan has demanded to sift all of you like wheat' (Lk 22:31); and again, in Mark 14:37: 'And he came and found them sleeping, and he said to Peter, "Simon, are you asleep? Could you not keep awake one hour?"' Jacob, the least successful at living up to his new name, continues – with a few exceptions – to be called 'Jacob' throughout the Genesis narrative. Jacob was born to strive, as all humans are, but – like many of us – he often took the easy option.

Rilke, heavily influenced by the Jacob story, wrote passionately about striving and surrender in the poem 'The Man Watching'. When I first read it, in Robert Bly's translation, I felt that shock of recognition that all great poetry produces – the feeling that this poem was speaking directly to me. The poem opens with an unforgettable description of an approaching storm, and then goes on:

> What we choose to fight is so tiny!
> What fights with us is so great!
> If only we would let ourselves be dominated as things do
> by some immense storm,
> we would become strong too, and not need names.
> When we win it's with small things,
> and the triumph itself makes us small.
> What is extraordinary and eternal does not want to be
> bent by us.
> I mean the Angel who appeared to the wrestlers of the
> Old Testament.

God remained faithful to the promises he made to Jacob, renewing them when Jacob finally got around to revisiting Bethel. Despite Jacob's manifest imperfections, God loved this tenacious, bull-headed man – much as he loved cantankerous old Jonah, who didn't hesitate to argue with him, and unpleasant Lot, whose only saving grace seemed to be that he didn't look back.

'I will not let you go', Jacob said to the angel. This is echoed much later in the Song of Solomon when the Bride says, 'I found him whom my soul loves, I held him and would not let him go' (Song 3:4). And, later again, Jesus, the Good Shepherd, will say of his flock, 'My sheep hear my voice. I know them and they follow me. I give them eternal life, and they will never perish. No one will snatch them out of my hand' (Jn 10:27, 28).

When we find ourselves on that dark and lonely battlefield, wrestling with God, we need to bear in mind that the outcome of the wrestling will determine whether we will receive God's blessing, and whether we will receive the strength to be reconciled with our past and our present, and with those we have wronged. If we prevail, we prevail over ourselves and our own Esaus – all those whom we have wronged in our lives, all those with whom we must make peace. We will know that we, too, are no longer Jacob, but Israel.

> Whoever was beaten by this Angel
> (who often simply declined the fight)
> went away proud and strengthened
> and great from that harsh hand,
> that kneaded him as if to change his shape.

Winning does not tempt that man.
This is how he grows: by being defeated, decisively,
by constantly greater beings.[8]

NOTES

1   John Donne, 'A Nocturnall upon S. Lucies Day', in H.J.C. Grierson (ed.), *Metaphysical Lyrics and Poems of the Seventeenth Century*, Oxford University Press, 1971, p. 114.

2   Harold S. Kushner, *Living a Life That Matters*, New York, Pan Books, 2003, p. 3, 5.

3   Ivan Illich, *The Right to Useful Unemployment*, London, Marion Boyars Publishers Ltd., 1996, p. 20.

4   R.S. Thomas, 'Kneeling', from *Poems*, London, Phoenix, 2002, p. 69.

5   Kushner, op. cit., p. 31, 32.

6   St Gregory the Great, *Homilies on Ezekiel*, Book 2, Chapter 2, pp. 12–13; reference given in an article by Athanasios Hatzopoulos, 'The Struggle for a Blessing', *The Ecumenical Review*, October 1996, accessed at Questia Online Library: www.questia.com.

7   Søren Kierkegaard, *Either/Or*, Penguin Classics, 1992, p. 479.

8   Rainer Maria Rilke, 'The Man Watching', translated by Robert Bly, from *The Rag and Bone Shop of the Heart*, Harper Perennial, 1993, p. 298.

8

THE SINGING STARS

DAVID AND JOB

Master, it is wonderful for us to be here!

Luke 9:33[1]

A GOD WHO DANCES

'If these Christians want me to believe in their god,' wrote Nietzsche in *Thus Spoke Zarathustra*, 'they'll have to sing better songs, they'll have to look more like people who have been saved, they'll have to wear on their countenance the joy of the beatitudes. I could only believe in a god who dances'.[2] His sentiments will strike a chord with many Christians.

I was one of the last generations of First Communicants to have a Tridentine Missal. It had a white shiny cover like mother-of-pearl, and 1,465 flimsy pages. The Ordinary of the Mass was printed in two columns, Latin on the left and English on the right. At last I had the key to this mysterious language and I followed it avidly. As soon as the celebrant began the 'Mass of the Catechumens', I was following the English translation: 'I will go in unto the altar of God.' To which the altar server replied, 'Unto God, who gives joy to my youth'.

I found this exchange puzzling. The God of my youth had little to do with joy and everything to do with judgement and penance. The Church of my youth was a house of prayer, of awe and majesty, but never of celebration. This was a Church of 'solemnities' rather than of 'feast days' – indeed, any notion of festivity and celebration was effectively suppressed by the heavy description 'holy days of obligation'. The liturgy was at its richest and most dramatic in the fasting seasons of Lent and Advent. There were no Christmas trees in our churches then, or harvest baskets, or colourful montages by First Communion and Confirmation classes. The brightest events seemed to be the Marian feasts – the crowning of the Queen of the May and the May processions.

It was in the great requiem Masses and in the pageantry of Holy Week that the Church seemed to come into its own. I can still hear the subdued thunder of the organ, the terrifying rhythms of the 'Dies Irae', the militant 'Faith of our Fathers', the haunting Tenebrae – 'service of the shadows'. I can still see the eerie humped shapes of the statues shrouded in the colours of mourning in Holy Week, the gaping tabernacle on Good Friday. I can smell the air, heavy with incense in the nave, close and stifling in the cramped confessional. The church was a holy place, majestic, awe-inspiring, a sombre theatre of unending war against the forces of darkness. Every Sunday, I left the church with the chilling lines of the last prayer of the Mass, the prayer to St Michael the Archangel, ringing in my ears: '... do thou, prince of the heavenly host, by the power of God thrust down to hell Satan and all wicked spirits, who wander through the world for the ruin of souls.' Church penitential, Church militant, Church triumphant – but never Church jubilant.

Then came Pope John XXIII and *Aggiornamento*; Pope Paul VI and the new rite in the vernacular. I entered enthusiastically into the era of the Folk Mass, and years later regretted the passing of ritual and ceremony that evoked such a sense of God's mystery and majesty. Throughout all that time, I never quite overcame the early sense of not quite belonging in a church. Churches, for me, were a place where I was a hushed spectator rather than an enthusiastic participant – a place in which to consider one's shortcomings rather than be embraced in God's love; high on theatre, but low on spiritual energy.

Then, one Lenten Sunday, a phrase from the Gospel struck me like a thunderbolt. It was Peter, speaking on Mount Tabor after the Transfiguration of Christ: 'Master,' he cried, 'it is wonderful for us to be here!' (Lk 9:33).[3] Yet here I was, like Peter, in the presence of God, but feeling no sense of wonder. I listened each Sunday to the words of Christ but could not identify with those who listened to him in the Temple, described in Mark 12:37: 'the large crowd was listening to him with delight.' Delight and wonder, in short, were conspicuously absent from my perception of God. My worship was joyless, my 'Amen' was said lifelessly. I could accept, intellectually, that God might possibly delight in me, but I did not see that it might be appropriate for me to reciprocate! It took a visit to 2 Samuel and 1 Chronicles to see how exultant one might be in the presence of God – at that time represented by the Ark of the Covenant.

'AND THE SANCTUARY RESOUNDED FROM EARLY MORNING'

When the prophet Samuel came to live with Eli the high priest, the Ark of the Covenant had been in the Tabernacle at Shiloh, in the hill country of Ephraim, for over three centuries. In the time of the Judges, Shiloh was the capital of Israel. War had been raging with the Philistines for several generations and, shortly before Samuel anointed King David, the Ark was lost to the Philistines in the course of a disastrous battle. It was eventually returned to Israel and remained at Kiriath-jearim in Judah for twenty years.

When David's reign began, Israel had been at war with the Philistines for generations. In addition, the country was riven by civil war for several years following David's anointing by Samuel, as he had to contend with the tribes supporting Saul's son Ish–boshet. His kingdom was confined to Judah in southern Israel, and he ruled from Hebron, where Abraham, Sarah, Isaac and Jacob were buried. Following his defeat of Ish-boshet, 'all the tribes of Israel came to David at Hebron, and said, "Look, we are your bone and flesh ... The Lord said to you: it is you who shall be shepherd of my people Israel, you who shall be ruler over Israel" ... and they anointed David king over Israel' (2 Sam 5:1, 3).

Now, with all twelve tribes accepting his rulership, David sought a more central base from which to govern. He decided on Jerusalem, which was ideally placed in non-tribal territory between north and south. Its strategic importance was immense; it is situated in a pivotal position at the crossroads of the east–west trade route linking the Transjordan with the Mediterranean Sea, and the Ridge Road ('The Patriarch's Highway') that ran from Shechem to Hebron. Then called Jebus, the city was in the hands of the Jebusites, a remnant Canaanite tribe that had heavily fortified the city. 'David and Israel marched to Jerusalem, that is, Jebus where the Jebusites were, the inhabitants of the land' (1 Chr 11:4). Having captured Jerusalem, David went on to achieve a decisive defeat of the Philistines.

David inaugurated Israel's political golden age. From the small city of Jerusalem (about fifteen acres in size in David's time) he transformed a tribal people – not many generations removed from slavery – into a powerful and organised state, stretching from Damascus in the north to the Red Sea in the south, and from the Arabian Desert in the east to the Mediterranean in the west. Bringing the Ark of the Covenant to his city was key to David's establishment of Jerusalem as Israel's religious and political capital. He brought it with wild, unadulterated delight as described in 2 Samuel 6:12-15:

> So David went and brought up the ark of God from the house of Obed-Edom to the city of David with rejoicing; and when those who bore the ark of the Lord had gone six paces, he sacrificed an ox and a fatling. David danced before the Lord with all his might; David was girded with a linen ephod. So David and all the house of Israel brought up the ark of the Lord with shouting, and with the sound of the trumpet.

David's haughty wife Michal, Saul's daughter, was disgusted. 'How the King of Israel honoured himself today,' she observed sarcastically, 'uncovering himself today before the eyes of his servants' maids, as any vulgar fellow might shamelessly uncover himself!' (2 Sam 6:20)

David, unabashed, replied to Michal that he was dancing for the Lord and not for the onlookers – the Lord 'who chose me in place of your father and all his household to appoint me as prince over Israel ... I will make myself yet more contemptible than this, and I will be abased in my own eyes; but by the maids of whom you have spoken, by them I shall be held in honour' (2 Sam 6:21, 22). 1 Chronicles 15 repeats the story, with more musical elaboration:

> The Levites carried the ark of God on their shoulders with the poles, as Moses had commanded according to the word of the Lord. David also commanded the chiefs of the Levites to appoint their kindred as the singers to play on musical instruments, on harps and lyres and cymbals, to raise loud sounds of joy ... David was clothed with a robe of fine linen, as also were all the Levites who were carrying the ark, and the singers, and Chenaniah the leader of the music of the singers; and David wore a linen ephod ... So all Israel brought up the ark of the covenant of the Lord with shouting, to the sound of the horn, trumpets, and cymbals, and made loud music on harps and lyres.

In this way, David established a new kind of musical worship – unceasing jubilant praise in front of the tent which housed the Ark. The Book of Sirach says of David:

> In all that he did he gave thanks to the Holy One, the Most High, proclaiming his glory;
> he sang praise with all his heart, and he loved his Maker.
> He placed singers before the altar,

to make sweet melody with their voices.
He gave beauty to the feasts,
and arranged their times throughout the year,
while they praised God's holy name,
and the sanctuary resounded from early morning.
(Sir 47:8-10)

Our sanctuaries, unlike the tent – and later the temple – of the Ark, no longer 'resound from early morning'. When did any of us ever think to praise God with 'dancing and leaping' as David did? When did we last sing and make melody to the Lord with all our heart as Paul recommends in his letter to the Ephesians (5:19)? Or 'clap our hands' or 'shout for joy' as the Psalmist urges (Ps 47:1; 37:4)? We tend to regard this kind of worship as primitive, outmoded. Although we were created body and soul, modern man is *disembodied* in his ritual.

The cosmic dance

Laughter and play are conspicuous in their absence from our worship, despite the fact that we were created playful. Indeed, Wisdom – the first of all creation and God's endless delight according to Proverbs (8:22-31) – is described in these terms:

God created me, first-fruits of his fashioning, before the
oldest of his works ...
When he fixed the heavens firm, I was there ...
when he traced the foundations of the earth,
I was beside the master craftsman,
delighting him day after day,
ever at play in his presence,

at play everywhere on his earth,
delighting to be with the children of men.[4]

If we are indeed created in God's image, then our human play is rooted in divine play. Every creature plays, especially the young – from kittens and puppies to bullocks and tiger cubs. As children we play with joyful abandon, delighting our parents as Wisdom delighted God day after day. But in our churches, the child in us is stifled. Worship for many of us is a thing of leaden seriousness; for our children it is all too often an incomprehensible tedium. If anyone shouted with delight in the presence of the Lord in the tabernacle, the Ark of our times, they would be put out of the church very quickly. Yet it is the child in us who can most truly live in a state of becoming – untrammelled by the past, always open to growth and change. It is the child in us who can sense what Meister Eckhart calls the perfection and stability of eternity, where there is neither time nor space, neither before nor after, 'but everything present in one new, fresh-springing now where millenniums last no longer than the twinkling of an eye'.[5]

It is the child in us who can truly be open to God's constant invitation to be born again, to be part of the creation which is itself constantly being recreated. It is the child in us who can thrill to a sense of closeness to the source of all creation. Without a sense of wonder, our praise of God will be sterile.

Thomas Merton draws an extraordinary picture of God playing in the garden of his own creation and adds:

> If we could let go of our own obsession with what we think is the meaning of it all, we might be able to hear

His call and follow Him in His mysterious cosmic dance. We do not have to go very far to catch echoes of that game, and of that dancing. When we are alone on a starlit night ... when we see children in a moment when they are really children; when we know love in our hearts ... at such times the awakening, the turning inside out of all values, the 'newness', the emptiness and the purity of vision that make themselves evident, provide a glimpse of the cosmic dance.

According to Merton, the more we try to analyse life, the more we involve ourselves in sadness. 'But it does not matter much because *no* despair of ours can alter the reality of things, or stain the joy of the cosmic dance which is always there. Indeed, we are in the midst of it, and it is in the midst of us, for it beats in our very blood, whether we want it to or not.'[6]

It may beat in our blood, but we still deny it. It is too easy to live in the created world as though in a transparent capsule – seeing, but feeling no sense of identity with, creation. There have been so many times when I have felt no real sense of being constantly in the Creator's presence, let alone *belonging* there; no sense of interconnectedness with the rest of creation. I glided along the surface of the spinning earth, never listening to its heartbeat. I looked into the depths of the universe, and never heard the singing of the stars. Unlike the Psalmist, I never saw the mountains skipping like rams (Ps 114:6) or watched the wilderness bloom. I lived beside the sea, but without sharing the Psalmist's wonder at its vast expanses teeming with countless creatures, creatures both great and small; 'there go the ships, and Leviathan that you formed to sport in it' (Ps 104:26).

David was completely connected with the created world. It pervades his psalms and it shines through the great song of praise which he sings after dancing and making merry before the Ark:

> Let the heavens be glad, and let the earth rejoice;
> let them say among the nations, 'The Lord is king!'
> Let the sea roar, and all that fills it;
> let the field exult, and everything in it;
> Then shall the trees of the forest sing for joy before the
> Lord ...
> O give thanks to the Lord, for he is good;
> for his steadfast love endures for ever!

All the assembled people cry 'Amen' to this explosion of hope and gratitude (1 Chr 16:31-36).

GOD'S CREATIVE FORCE

It took David to show me how I might more appropriately praise God. For a depiction of God's exuberant creative force, it took the book of long-suffering Job to make the hair stand on the back of my neck. The book of Job is generally held to be the oldest book in the Bible. It was circulated orally in the second millennium BC and written down in Hebrew at roughly the time of David and Solomon. The historical Job is believed to have lived long before Moses.

In the Bible, Job is a wealthy and God-fearing man living a semi-nomadic life with his large and happy family. Revered in the community and contented in his domestic life, Job looks forward to a comfortable old age. God speaks admiringly of his goodness to Satan, who tartly replies that Job has no reason not to be good: 'But stretch out your hand now, and touch his bone and his flesh, and he will curse you to your face.' (Job 2:5) God agrees to allow Job's faith to be tried and Job accordingly experiences a series of terrible disasters in which he loses his entire family and all his wealth. His body is afflicted with a loathsome disease and this once highly respected man becomes a figure of mockery.

Through the arguments of Job's friends and through Job's own words, the book explores the dilemma of how a loving God permits human suffering. No resolution to the problem is found in any of these arguments. In a heartbreaking discourse, Job recalls his past happiness. He begins:

> Oh that I were as in the months of old,
> as in the days when God watched over me;
> when his lamp shone over my head,
> and by his light I walked through darkness;
> as I was in my prime,
> when the friendship of God was upon my tent;
> when the Almighty was still with me,
> when my children were around me. (Job 29:2-5)

He goes on to outline in detail his past contentment and how he used to think, 'I shall die in my nest, and I shall multiply my days like sand, my roots spread out to the waters'. He then depicts his current misery: his soul is poured out within him; the night racks his bones; pain gnaws him incessantly. 'I am a brother of jackals,' he exclaims, 'and a companion of ostriches.' (Job 30:29)

His friends insist on the orthodox explanation, that Job's sufferings must be a retribution for personal wrongdoing, and they urge Job to repent. Job utterly rejects this explanation. He has explored every possible way in which he could conceivably have sinned, and drawn a blank in each case. In a wonderful verse, this formidable man threatens the Creator with his own non-existence: 'Why have you made me your mark? ...Why do you not pardon my transgression ...? For now I shall lie in the earth; you will seek me, but I shall not be' (Job 7:20, 21).

Job steadfastly refuses to curse God, but his sense of injury and outrage build up to a furious climax in which he demands to see God and question him face to face about the justice of his actions:

> I will say to God, 'Do not condemn me;
> let me know why you contend against me.
> Does it seem good to you to oppress,
> to despise the work of your hands,
> and favour the schemes of the wicked?
> Do you have eyes of flesh?
> Do you see as humans see?
> Are your days like the days of mortals,
> or your years like human years,
> that you seek out my iniquity,
> and search for my sin,
> although you know that I am not guilty,
> and there is no one to deliver out of your hand?'
> (Job 10:2-7)

As a passionate demand for an answer to the perennial question 'why do good people suffer?' it is hard to equal. 'Let me alone,' he concludes indignantly, 'that I may find a little comfort before I go, never to return, to the land of gloom and chaos.' (Job 10:20-22)

The 'miserable comforters' continue to urge their point of view, but Job becomes increasingly impatient with them. 'I am not inferior to you!' he exclaims. 'I would speak to the Almighty and I desire to argue my case with God.' (Job 13:3) While his friends continue to protest at his presumption, Job – in all his wretched state – goes from strength to strength, confident that if God would allow him to put his case, he would be acquitted. 'When he has tested me, I shall come out like gold.' (23:10) Like Jonah, he is not afraid to speak his mind to God.

His discourses conclude with a ringing demand for justice: 'Oh, that I had one to hear me! (Here is my signature! Let the Almighty answer me!)' (31:35) There is nothing submissive about Job's cry: 'signature' literally means 'taw', the last letter in the Hebrew alphabet. This is Job saying: 'This is my last word. Answer me!'

And the Almighty *does* respond to this audacious demand, in a sublime poem that lasts four chapters (38-41). In sweeping verse he presents a series of questions to Job, asking where he was when God created the earth, the tumultuous sea, the dawn 'grasping the earth by its skirts', the gates of night, the elements and the constellations, all animals and living things. The language is magnificent, conveying a sense of beauty, majesty, mystery and power that has hardly been equalled in the thousands of years since it was written. The first time I really experienced Scripture as inspired writing was when I first encountered the Book of Job.

'Where were you,' God asks Job, 'when I laid the foundation of the earth? ... When the morning stars sang together, and all the sons of God shouted for joy?' 'Who shut in the sea with doors, when it burst forth from the womb; when I made clouds its garment, and thick darkness its swaddling band?' 'Have the gates of death been revealed to you?' 'Have you entered the storehouses of the snow?' 'Can you bind the chains of the Pleiades, or loose the cords of Orion?'

And so it goes on, this extraordinary journey through the created universe, question after question, with the refrain: 'I will question you and you will declare to me. Will you put me in the wrong? Will you condemn me that you may be justified?' In an abrupt change of tone, God conjures up two less recognisable entities. Can Job tame the Behemoth, God asks, the colossal creature whose bones are like tubes of bronze and whose limbs are like bars of iron? Or can he catch the gigantic sea monster Leviathan, out of whose mouth flame leaps? It is quite clear from the description of these creatures that they represent far more than the hippopotamus or the crocodile with which they have been associated. In Jewish belief, Behemoth is the primal unconquerable monster of the land, as Leviathan is the primal monster of the waters of the sea. They often symbolise evil – in the Book of Revelation the beast from the sea and the beast from the land are symbols of brute force and sensuality, given power and authority by Satan (Rev 13).

Can you capture the Leviathan and make it serve you? God asks Job. Can you tame it? Play with it? If you cannot, how do you dare to confront your God, who is immeasurably greater than Leviathan? God gives no verbal answer to Job's question as to why the innocent are permitted to suffer, nor does he see why he should. He does not 'owe' Job an explanation: 'Who has given to me, that I should repay him? Whatever is under the whole heaven is mine.' (Job 41:11)[7]

> God has not justified Job, but he has come to him personally; the upholder of the universe cares for a lonely man so deeply that he offers him the fullness of his communion. Job is not vindicated but he has obtained far more than a recognition of his innocence: he has been accepted by the ever-present master-worker, and intimacy with the Creator makes vindication superfluous. The philosophical problem is not solved, but it is transfigured by the theological reality of the divine-human rapport.[8]

All that is left is for Job to accept the inscrutable grace of the God whose thoughts are not our thoughts, nor his ways our ways, 'For as the heavens are higher than the earth, so are my ways higher than your ways' (Is 55:8, 9).

WRESTING A RESPONSE FROM GOD

'I had heard of you by the hearing of the ear,' Job says to God, 'but now my eye sees you.' Martin Buber saw this as God's answer to Job:

> Through the intensity of his 'turning,' through his demand that God speak to him, [Job] receives a revelation of God such as could not otherwise be his. It is 'just at the height of Job's trial ... just in the midst of

the terror of the other, the incomprehensible, ununderstandable works, just from out of the secret,' that God's ways of working are revealed. Job accuses God of injustice and tries in vain to penetrate to Him through the divine remoteness. Now God draws near Job and Job 'sees' Him. It is this nearness to God, following His apparent hiddenness, which is God's answer to the suffering Job as to why he suffers – an answer which is understandable only in terms of the relationship itself.[9]

The conclusion of the story is brief and in prose, as Job's fortunes are restored and he dies 'an old man, and full of days'.

After the soaring verse of the preceding chapters, the ending seems almost formulaic, a ritual tidying up of all the loose ends. The temptation is to race through the last two paragraphs, but to do this is to risk missing the significance of two critical verses in which God speaks to Job's misguided friends: 'My wrath is kindled against you ... for you have not spoken of me what is right, as my servant Job has' (42:7) and again, 'I will accept [Job's] prayer not to deal with you according to your folly; for you have not spoken of me what is right, as my servant Job has done' (42:8). These two verses celebrate Job's directness with God. It was Job's plain speaking and determination which wrested that mighty response from God. Like blunt-spoken Jonah he did not hesitate to engage honestly with God. There was not a shred of false humility in their engagement; these were men in whom – as Jesus would later say admiringly of Nathaniel – there was no guile. They spoke what was on their mind and God honoured them for it.

It seems a relatively simple thing to do, but it isn't. Which of us has not been haunted at some time or other by the fear that everything we believe is a delusion – the stuff of a fable told to a child to allay his fear of the dark? How often have we acknowledged that fear to ourselves, let alone to God? Or the many other terrors, resentments, hatred and guilt that drain our lives of joy and hope? If we are to mend something that is broken, we must first be able to look at the break. Job described his own wretchedness pitilessly, in words that resonate with us four thousand years later. It is all here, the absence and the silence of God, the prosperity of the wicked, the broken spirit, the raging against fate. But underlying it all is the refusal to give up, the refusal to be silent – the same capacity of endurance that marked the most flawed of the biblical protagonists. Even before God succumbs to this relentless battering at his door, Job can express hope. In this, the Bible's oldest book, the gloom and desolation of Sheol is displaced by the first expression of belief in life after death:

> For I know that my Redeemer lives,
> and that at the last he will stand upon the earth;
> and after my skin has been thus destroyed,
> then in my flesh I shall see God. (Job 19:25, 26)

NOTES

1   From the *New Jerusalem Bible* (NJB).

2   As translated by Thomas Common and accessed at:
www.gutenberg.org.

3   NJB.

4   NJB.

5   Meister Eckhart, *Sermon: Contemplations, hints and promises,*
originally in Franz Pfeiffer, *Meister Eckhart,* translated by C. Evans,
Whitefish, MT., Kessinger Publications, 1924, accessed at:
www.geocities.com/Athens/Acropolis/5164/ eckhart.htm.

6   Thomas Merton, OCSO, *New Seeds of Contemplation,* New York,
Penguin Books/New Directions Paperback, 1972, pp. 296–7.

7   This is from the RSV translation and is also similar to the NJB
version; the NRSV does not follow the same interpretation.

8   From the notes to Job 42 in the *New Oxford Annotated Bible,* Oxford
University Press, 1971, p. 654.

9   Maurice S. Friedman, *Martin Buber: The Life of Dialogue,* London,
Routledge, 2002, p. 301.

THE DARKEST JOURNEY

Simon of Cyrene

And as they led him away, they seized a man, Simon of Cyrene, who was coming from the country, and they laid the cross on him, and made him carry it behind Jesus.

Luke 23:26

'My God, my God, why abandonest thou me?'

I remember the rain, the dark, the quiet. The open window and the rain falling like comfort. I listened to her breathing and watched her – the skeletal body with the powerful heart, the heart that would not let her die. Her hand, so beautiful still, lay on the smooth cover of the bed. And the rain falling, falling, falling.

My mother could no longer swallow. I had a supply of small sponges which I used to moisten her parched lips. In that sickroom, where the shadow of Calvary cast such a deep shadow, the resonance of the gesture was inescapable. I recalled the sponge full of vinegar on the end of the hyssop branch, held to the mouth of the crucified Jesus. Another, even older voice, sounded in my ears: 'I am weary with my crying; my throat is parched. My eyes grow dim with waiting for my God.' (Ps 69:3) Three times before she sank into the final coma, she whispered, 'My God, my God, why abandonest thou me?'

These were the final hours of a protracted illness. My mother had been a beautiful, energetic and gregarious woman, with many interests. She was a daily Mass-goer throughout her long life and really lived her faith. Her house and her heart were always open to anyone in need, and she radiated encouragement and hope. It was only in her later years that I came to know that the hope she gave to others was not often something she experienced herself. The seemingly unshakeable faith was built on quicksand. 'I don't know if I believe in God or in an afterlife', she told me many years before she became ill. However, she continued to practise her religion and there were very few among her large circle of friends who suspected how much her faith was a willed thing and not a gift from God.

Then a series of falls occurred, leading to serious injuries – a nasty wrist fracture from one, a fractured hip from another. A lengthy period of rehabilitation followed, during which she showed great courage, grace, remarkable good cheer and a complete lack of self-pity. She had another fall, broke her pelvis in two places, and did not walk again. A series of mini strokes followed; she then fractured her other hip and never recovered. Far worse, however, than her physical ailments was the protracted mental anguish which she suffered in her final years. She became possessed by an unrelenting terror of death which increased dramatically in her final illness. Throughout her last seven weeks I sat with her many hours each day, doing what I could to comfort her.

'My God, my God, why abandonest thou me?' The archaic language was that of her childhood. When she reached for a concept of God, it was the God of her far off schooldays – an Old Testament God of judgement and retribution. Her religion, practised so faithfully over so many years, brought her no solace. No glimmer of comfort could touch her. This kind, warm-hearted and good-living woman dreaded going into the darkness. In that small room, I watched her world contract. Terror filled her mind to the exclusion of almost any other emotion. Yet, when I arrived in her room, she never failed to recognise me. Her eyes became a blazing glory of love. All her former strength and hope lived once more in that shining gaze. Then the darkness took hold of her again. And of me. Together, we took her cross up again.

THE MAN FROM 'THE HOLE IN THE HEAVENS'

It was there, in that quiet room, that I came to know Simon of Cyrene. I gazed across the space of two millennia and saw him, another person bent under a cross not his own. Another person on a seemingly hopeless journey.

Cyrene was an ancient Greek colony, beautifully set in a fertile valley beneath the wooded uplands of Jebel Akhdar in what is now north-east Libya. The city of Cyrene gave its name to the surrounding region, Cyrenaica, a name retained to this day. The seventh-century BC Greeks who settled Cyrenaica, fleeing drought in their home island of Thera (modern Santorini), were directed to this spot by Berber tribesmen who told them that there was a 'hole in the heavens' here. Through this 'hole' abundant and life-giving rain fell to create a lush expanse in the wastes of the Sahara. Cyrenaica was fertile enough to supply a million bushels of grain to famine-stricken areas on the Greek islands and mainland in 390 BC. By the time Simon of Cyrene was born, Cyrenaica had come under Roman rule. The name 'Simon' is the Greek form of a typically Jewish name – Shimon or Shimeon, 'he who hears'. The names of his two sons (see Mk 15:21) are quite another matter. Alexander and Rufus were quite unusual names for Jewish children. They reflect, respectively, the Greek and Roman influences in Cyrenaica and they suggest that Simon was very comfortable with the other cultures in his home town. He may well have been a wealthy Hellenised Jew – devout enough to want to make the long pilgrimage to Jerusalem, but nonetheless living an assimilated, cosmopolitan life in his native Cyrene.

Now this Jewish Cyrenean is standing on the road to Golgotha, caught up in the melee of the crucifixion procession. The flat of a Roman spear is placed on his shoulder: under Roman law, soldiers had the right to press local people who were not Roman citizens into limited service without their consent (Jesus was probably referring to this when he urged, at the Sermon on the Mount: 'If anyone forces you to go one mile, go with him two miles.' (Mt 5:41))

It is not quite clear from the gospels whether Simon helped Jesus carry the cross, or whether Simon carried it himself. Matthew and Mark suggest the latter; Luke says Simon carried the cross 'behind Jesus' and John says Jesus 'went out bearing his own cross'. The general perception falls somewhere in the middle of these accounts: that Jesus went out carrying the cross but that the soldiers, afraid that Jesus would die before reaching Calvary, forced Simon either to help Jesus or carry the cross for him. We can be certain that Simon did not welcome his humiliating task. Yet at this moment in time, all unknowing, Simon – like the founders of his native city seven centuries earlier – is standing under 'a hole in the heavens'. The blood and sweat which rain down on him will transform his life. One would have expected Simon to put the memory of his horrible experience behind him as quickly as possible, but his two sons, Alexander and Rufus, will become sufficiently prominent in the young Christian Church to be mentioned by Mark and Paul (Mk 15:21; Rom 16:13). In shouldering his distasteful burden, it seems that Simon discovered that sometimes it is enough just to be in Christ's presence: 'I was found by those who did not seek me. I have shown myself to those who did not ask for me.' (Rom 10:20; Isa 65:1)

Just at this point of Simon's journey, however, there can be no glimpse of what is to come. The journey from Jerusalem to Calvary begins and ends in darkness. The suffering is unmitigated, the sadness unrelieved. Christ's own words from the cross seem to be a cry of despair. 'My God, my God, why hast thou forsaken me?'

THE UNLIT JOURNEY

As I sat with my mother though those pitiless days, I longed for some hint of deliverance, some faint intimation of the Easter that lay beyond Good Friday. I longed for it for myself as well as for her. I couldn't bear to see her go into unrelieved darkness. Had her lifetime of religious observance been a hollow thing, an elaborate construct to keep the darkness at bay? When she slept, I cast about in my mind for possible readings for her funeral. Verses from Ecclesiastes rang down the hollow corridors of my mind:

> When the doors on the street are shut; and the sound of the grinding is low, and one rises up at the voice of a bird, and all the daughters of song are brought low; when one is afraid of heights, and terrors are in the road; the almond tree blossoms, and the grasshopper drags itself along, and desire fails; because all must go to their eternal home, and the mourners will go about the streets: before the silver cord is snapped, and the golden bowl is broken, and the pitcher is broken at the fountain, and the wheel broken at the cistern, and the dust returns to the earth as it was, and the spirit returns to God who gave it.
> Vanity of vanities, says the Teacher. All is vanity!
> (Eccl 12:4-7)

'In the darkness ... I call, I cling, I want, and there is no one to answer ... I am told God lives in me – and yet the reality of darkness and coldness and emptiness is so great that nothing touches my soul.' I read these words with a shock of recognition. They are from the posthumously published letters of Mother Teresa of Calcutta and they shed a completely new light on a woman whom some described as 'intoxicated with God'. Her letters reveal that throughout 1946 and 1947 Mother Teresa experienced a profound union with Christ. Then, as soon as her mission with the destitute began, the voice of God became silent in her life and she never heard it again in the fifty years which followed. This smiling saint radiated joy while in her heart she experienced

> ... just that terrible pain of loss, of God not wanting me, of God not being God, of God not really existing ... People say they are drawn close to God – seeing my strong faith. Is this not deceiving people? Every time I have wanted to tell the truth – that I have no faith – the words just do not come – my mouth remains closed. And yet I still keep on smiling at God and all.[1]

> The whole time smiling – Sisters and people pass such remarks – they think my faith, trust and love are filling my very being ... Could they but know how my cheerfulness is the cloak by which I cover the emptiness and misery.[2]

Even when her interior life was most arid, Mother Teresa forced herself to her knees and prayed, although the prayer may have been no more than mechanical repetition. 'What else is the beating of the heart but repetition?' asks theologian Romano Guardini. 'What else is breathing but a repetition? Always the same in and out; but by breathing we live ...'[3]

She plodded on, as Simon plodded on with the cross. Neither had asked for this particular burden but, as Simon's life was transformed by this bleak journey, Mother Teresa came to say, 'I have begun to love my darkness for I believe now that it is a part, a very small part, of Jesus' darkness and pain on earth'.[4] The words 'I thirst' are displayed alongside the Crucifix in all houses of Mother Teresa's order as a constant reminder of Christ's thirst as man and as God. Through her own interior darkness she participated in the thirst of Jesus, in his painful and burning longing for love. Also displayed in each chapel of Mother Teresa's order is an image of St Thérèse of Lisieux, another who thirsted for God in the desert of her soul's dark night, and who wrote:

> The darkness says mockingly to me, 'you believe that one day you will walk out of this fog that surrounds you! Advance, advance; rejoice in death which will give you not what you hope for but a night still more profound, the night of nothingness'.[5]

The sisters of Thérèse's community and her early biographers suppressed or played down mention of her spiritual desolation, no doubt thinking it at odds with the conventional face of sanctity. The 'thick darkness' which Thérèse entered during Easter 1896 lasted until her death in September the following year. Thérèse experienced a moment of respite a few days before she died. She felt herself pierced by a burning ray of fire, but wrote:

> I have experienced it only this once and for a single moment; then I quickly fell back into my usual aridity ... Do not think that I am overwhelmed with consolations. Far from it! My joy consists in being deprived of all joy here on earth.[6]

There was no respite for my mother. She brought me into the world and I, bent under the weight of her cross, held her in my arms as she left it. Her journey was unlit to the end. Or so it seemed to me. Thérèse saw her crisis of faith as an opportunity to offer her sufferings to open Heaven to unbelievers. While sharing the darkness of atheism, she lived by the light of a willed faith. Mother Teresa saw her desert of the soul as a way of quenching Christ's thirst for love. My mother didn't go willingly into the desert and, sitting by her bedside, I felt more in common with the ancient figure of Simon of Cyrene than I did with Thérèse and Teresa. There was no evident light for my mother on her last journey. No light for Simon of Cyrene. No light for Christ as he struggles to his place of execution. But the hill of Calvary is also an altar. The victim is also the priest: his death is simultaneously sacrificial and redemptive. When all seems lost, Christ can still say to the crucified thief, 'Truly, I say to you, today you will be with me in Paradise'.

I sat by my mother as Simon probably stood at the foot of the cross. Simon can have no reason to believe that he is seeing things any way other than they actually are. He is looking at a crucified man, hearing his cry of despair. He watches him die, with no alleviation of his suffering. He watches the breath go out of the crucified man and probably asks himself, as I was asking myself, 'what is it all for?' If Simon has just come in to Jerusalem, he is unlikely to have known much about Jesus. Certainly, he would not have met him or heard him teach. I kept thinking about the dim figures of Alexander and Rufus. If they had become committed Christians it must have been as a result of their father's brief encounter with Christ on that Good Friday. And I, who had encountered Christ countless times in the Eucharist, could sit by my mother on her Good Friday and not see any Easter Sunday beyond.

TRAVELLING SAFELY IN THE NIGHT

I listen again with Simon to that terrible cry from the cross: 'My God, my God, why hast thou forsaken me?' This time I listen somewhat differently. I place Good Friday in the context of Easter Sunday and I place Christ's words in the context in which they were written. They are the opening words of Psalm 22, and any devout Jew at the foot of the cross would have known how the Psalm continued. It goes on to describe in graphic detail the nature of the death the Messiah will undergo, and it ends with the ringing proclamation, 'Posterity will serve him; future generations will be told about the Lord, and proclaim his deliverance to a people yet unborn'. Far from being a cry of despair, it is a shout of triumph. Simon's journey, like Christ's, is ending and beginning. Mother Teresa's words could have resonated as easily with Simon as they did with me: 'It does not matter what you feel, but what he feels in you ... you and I must let him live in us and through us in the world.'[7]

Christ is the new temple of God, the place where God dwells. About two hundred years before Simon was born, another Cyrenean, Jason of Cyrene, wrote the second book of Maccabees for Diaspora Jews in Egypt, informing them about the restoration of the Temple and urging them to make the annual pilgrimage to Jerusalem. All unknowing, Simon – who has come to make the pilgrimage to the Temple – is witnessing the end of the old Temple and the beginning of the new. As Christ dies on the cross, the veil of the Temple in Jerusalem is rent in two. It is a highly symbolic event. The veil was the barrier which separated the Holy of Holies from the rest of the Temple, preventing the people from entering God's presence. Now, the way into God's presence is opened by Christ's death.

As I watched with my mother in the night, hoping for some sign of the rending of her veil, I recalled the words of another follower of the cross: 'The soul, though in darkness, travels securely.'[8] Describing this 'darkness', St John of the Cross (a writer much read by St Thérèse) in his great canticle *The Dark Night of the Soul* tells how the soul is brought low, becoming helpless and unsupported; the imagination is shackled; the memory is gone; the understanding is in darkness, unable to understand anything; and the will is arid and constrained. All the faculties are useless and, in addition to all this, a thick and heavy cloud covers the soul, keeping it in pain and seemingly far away from God. His description, written over four-hundred years earlier, described exactly what I was witnessing at my mother's bedside.

The words 'nothing, nothing, nothing' fill the pages of *The Dark Night of the Soul*. For John, nothingness meant 'sweeping away of images and thoughts of God to meet Him in the darkness and obscurity of pure faith which is above all concepts'.[9] I recalled the fuller context of John's words, as he went on to say:

> So when you see your desire obscured, your will arid and constrained, and your faculties incapable of any interior act, do not be afflicted by this, but consider it instead as a great happiness, since God is freeing you from yourself and taking the matter out of your hands. For with those hands, however well they may serve you, you could

never labour so effectively, so perfectly and so securely as now, when God takes your hand and guides you in the darkness, as though you were blind, along a road to a destination you do not know.[10]

Not only does the soul travel safely when it travels in this darkness, but it makes even greater progress. It may be going reluctantly along a road it doesn't know and may feel it is losing ground – but St John points out that if a traveller is to go to new and unknown lands he must take new roads, and make journeys unguided by his past experience:

> In the same way, when the soul is making most progress, it is travelling in darkness, knowing nothing. So, since God is the Master and Guide of this blind soul, it may well and truly rejoice, once it has learned to understand this, and say: 'In darkness and secure'.[11]

Like Simon, I was present under a 'hole in the heavens' without knowing it. What was falling into that room wasn't the rain which fell onto the desert in ancient Cyrenaica, nor the sweat and blood of Christ which fell upon Simon of Cyrene, but something as fruitful and redemptive as either. It was what John of the Cross described as the dark waters close to God in which the striving soul is hidden and protected:

> The soul, though in darkness, travels securely because of the courage it acquires as soon as it enters the dark, painful and gloomy waters of God. Though it is dark, still it is water, and it can only refresh and strengthen the

soul in all that is most necessary for it, though it does so painfully and in darkness ... Thus the soul goes forth out of itself, away from all created things to the sweet and delightful union of the love of God, in darkness and in safety.[12]

In that room, over those weeks, I came to realise that, as Mother Teresa said, what we *feel* is not always important. I prayed for the grace to place myself in Christ's presence and to endure. Slowly, I came to see that every moment of every day we, like Simon, stand under a 'hole in the heavens', if we will only look up. Jesus, before so many significant events, raised his eyes to heaven – before the miracle of the loaves and fishes, before healing the man born deaf and dumb, before raising Lazarus, and before instituting the sacrament of the Eucharist at the Last Supper.

DAWN WITHOUT DARKNESS

My mother's soul left her in the darkness before dawn four days after Good Friday. I held her in my arms as her powerful heart fought to the last. Then the rasping breath became suddenly quieter. There was a pause between breaths, then a longer pause. Finally, almost imperceptibly, she drew her last breath in this world and I whispered Christ's final prayer, 'Into thy hands I commit her spirit'. Christ's own words in turn echoed Psalm 31, Verse 5 and – almost like a response – the remaining part of that verse suddenly filled my ears, 'thou hast redeemed me, O Lord, faithful God'.

As I laid her back on the pillow, the dawn chorus broke outside. Birdsong poured though the open window. The sky was still black, night's density thinning only along the brim of the

horizon. This crescent of light would sweep around the earth from pole to pole with the dawn chorus accompanying it as it has for a million years. No matter how deep the night, the continuous movement of light and song is illuminating some part of the world. My mother had reached a dawn without darkness.

At her funeral, we didn't read Ecclesiastes' gloomy verses after all: we chose instead this passage from the Song of Solomon:

> Arise, my beloved, my beautiful one,
> and come!
>
> For see, the winter is past,
> the rains are over and gone.
>
> The flowers appear on the earth,
> the time of pruning the vines has come,
> and the song of the dove is heard in our land.
>
> The fig tree puts forth its figs,
> and the vines, in bloom, give forth fragrance.
> Arise, my beloved, my beautiful one,
> and come! (Song 2:10-13)[13]

NOTES

1   Mother Teresa and Brian Kolodiejchuk, *Come Be My Light*,
       Doubleday, 2007. Quotation taken from *Time* preview of the book in
       an article by Rev. Michael Van Der Peet, 'Mother Teresa's Crisis of
       Faith', 23 August 2007.

2   Cf. Fr A. Huart, SJ, 'Mother Teresa: Joy in the Night', *Review for
       Religious*, Vol. 60, No. 5 (September/October 2001), (quoted by Fr
       Raniero Cantalamessa in his second homily, Advent 2003 at the Papal
       Household).

3   Romano Guardini, *The Rosary of Our Lady,* Sophia Institute Press, 1989,
       accessed online at: www.themissionchurch.com/guardinirosary.htm.

4   Fr Joseph Neuner, SJ, 'On Mother Teresa's Charism', *Review for
       Religious*, Vol. 60, No. 5 (September/October 2001).

5   Thérèse of Lisieux, *Story of a Soul: The Autobiography of St Thérèse of
       Lisieux*, translated by John Clarke, Washington, ICS, 1996,
       pp. 211–3.

6   Ibid.

7   David Scott, *A Revolution Of Love: The Meaning Of Mother Teresa*,
       Chicago, Loyola Press, 2005, p. 155.

8   St John of the Cross, 'The Dark Night of the Soul', Book 11, Chapter
       16, from *The Collected Works of St John of the Cross,* translated by Kieran
       Kavanaugh, OCD and Otilio Rodriguez, OCD, Washington, ICS
       Publications, 1991, accessed online at: www.carmelite.com/saints/
       john/works/dn.htm.

9   Hans Waldenfels, *Absolute Nothingness: Foundations for a Buddhist–
       Christian Dialogue*, Mahaw, N.J., Paulist Press, 1980, p. 141.

10   St John of the Cross, op. cit.

11   Ibid.

12   Ibid.

13   NASB.